Pink is the Color of Empathy

Becoming a high-value person in a disconnected world

BY

VITAL GERMAINE

2nd EDITION

This book is protected under the copyright laws of the United States of America. No Part of this publication may be reproduced or transmitted in any form or by any means, electronic or mechanical, including photocopying, recording, or by an information storage or retrieval system, without written permission from the author.

Editor: Leslie Hoffman
Cover Design: AIM TO WIN
Interior Design: AIM TO WIN

Trade Paperback **ISBN**: 9798766497783

1. Personal Development
2. Mental and Emotional Health
3. Inspirational

Published by:

Printed in the United States of America

Vital Germaine
Copyright © November 2023 reserved

PINK IS THE COLOR OF EMPATHY

Becoming a high-value person in a disconnected world

PINK IS THE COLOR OF EMPATHY

Becoming a high-value person in a disconnected world

The highest form of knowledge is empathy, for it requires us to suspend our egos and live in another's world. ... It requires profound purpose larger than the self-kind of understanding.

Plato, *The Republic*

Introduction

Once upon a time I believed that high-value people were only those with status: influence, financial clout or network reach. I was wrong.

If we reframe the meaning of a high-value person, we elevate a lot of people who are undermined in society. That may include you. Some of those wealthy, influential people (influencers) may be of high value in certain areas, but not across the board. Maybe they provide very little emotional value to those they love; think of the overworked executive who has very little time and energy for the kids. That person is of very little emotional value; and money is not everything.

You can become a high-value person in any field: a stay home mom or dad with a net worth of zero, or a social network of just your dog or cat, and of course, Aunt Sally. It's about how you are helping, supporting, and understanding people.

Pink Is The Color Of Empathy was written with two objectives:
1. To help those experiencing mental and emotional health challenges get back on their feet.
2. To enable the reader to become a high-value human being with the ability to help and support those in need. How do I know you will become one through empathy? Because I've witnessed the impact empathy has on a deep psychological level, in particular,

when it comes to mental/emotional health. Empathy not only changes lives, but it also saves lives. It's an incredibly powerful way of saying that you care, which inspires confidence and trust in others.

Maybe the best news is that it can be taught and learned, which will fashion priceless, meaningful, and positive ripple effects.

Pink Is The Color Of Empathy will exponentially impact you on a personal and professional level.

PINK IS THE COLOR OF EMPATHY

Becoming a high-value person in a disconnected world

Empathy changes lives

Chapter 1
Oh no!

During a performance of Cirque du Soleil's, *Quidam*, I witnessed an extremely dire situation. I expected one of my colleagues might die. This moment happened while on the US tour, in an act called *Banquin*. It inspired me to truly analyze and better understand the unseen driving force that compels teams and groups of people to collectively reach higher.

The *Banquin* act consists of strong burly Russian guys literally tossing and hurling light-weight performers across the stage. It has similarities to acrobatic cheerleading. These highly agile acrobats defy death as they flip and twist through time and space. At times, they land only on a sturdy set of shoulders. This one specific moment in the act when I thought a friend might break her neck if not die, was when my Russian comrades created a three-man-high tower of talent and testosterone, ready to catch a *petite* Russian girl named Nadya. She weighed less than ninety-five pounds, elegantly clad in all white: short dress, stockings, and a short matching Marylin Monroe type wig.

As they propelled Nadya high into the air, she rotated with impeccable dexterity toward the catcher at the top of the human column. A highly precarious landing ensued each and every night... one foot fitting perfectly into the hand of, Vlad, extended above his head. Nadya's face would tower above the stage and audience by about twenty-five feet. A hard rotating stage glared back, daring her to test its painful rigidity should she fall. Only the worse-case scenario would invite serious harm.

What do you know? The worse-case scenario happened. Vlad's grip failed him. Nadya's foot slipped. She fell headfirst, backward toward the ground.

Oh no!

Chapter 2
Shocker

We all experience life-changing moments. The before and after versions in our life stories. This Cirque story was one of many potentially career-ending situations I had experienced.

In 2015 I experienced a very personal life-changing event. It instilled a profound desire to better understand the human experience. There are times in life when one must simply wear the shoes rather than trying to understand what the shoes of another person might feel like. There are times when imagining what the other person's shoes feel and fit like, can make the difference to that person and society, in particular, in this age of elevated mental and emotional health challenges.

The discoveries and learning I encountered as a result surprised me. They confirmed everything I'd already felt, witnessed, believed in, doubted, or had denied, regarding humans.

Humans desperately needed more love, care and belonging. The world was far too emotionally disconnected. It desperately craved empathy. The findings as to why and the consequences thereof, shocked me.

The term empathy can be misleading, sometimes viewed as a weakness. It's a superpower. But only when correctly implemented. It's shared and needed in varying degrees at different times. Nonetheless, we all need it.

The first records of the word *empathy* come from the late 1800s from the context of psychology. The word comes from a translation of the German term *Einfühlung*, which literally means "a feeling in." It ultimately derives from the Greek *empátheia*, meaning "affection" or "passion," from e*m-*, meaning "in," and *path-*, the base of a verb meaning "to suffer."

– Dictionary.com

Our modern world has become more disconnected than ever. Empathy is the key to helping us build meaningful relationships with a strong and deep connection. We all need it. We all crave it. When we give it, everything changes. What if you could change lives, by positively impacting those you care for? What if you could save a life?

In the book *Greenlights*, a memoir by Matthew McConaughey, he shares a compelling story that illustrates the simplicity and power of empathy when effectively gifted to a person in need.

PINK IS THE COLOR OF EMPATHY

Becoming a high-value person in a disconnected world

At the time, Matthew McConaughey was experiencing real fame after being labelled "the next best thing" on the front page of a prominent magazine. The fame got to him. He felt lost, confused and in desperate need of direction and composure.

"I need a spiritual realignment," he declared.

He'd read about the Monastery of Christ located in the middle of a desert on the banks of the Chama River in New Mexico.

"I need to talk about some things going on in my life," he said to the Brother that greeted him.

The lending ear recommended a man by the name of Brother Christian. He would help McConaughey address and resolve his needs.

They went for a long walk in the desert. For the next three and a half hours Matthew revealed his demons in great depth. Brother Christian said nothing, only listened.

Another thirty minutes of walking went by. Still no comment from Brother Christian. McConaughey ended his confession in tears awaiting judgment.

Brother Christian broke his silence, uttering only two words. Those two words sum up the impact and power of empathy. The power of empathy, or caring without saying anything, yet letting somebody know you are there with and for them is what I finally understood to be an unspoken character trait that allowed Cirque performers to thrive and reach higher. It's what gives courage and daring to the likes of Nadya and us Cirque folk to do what we do. It's what gives everybody courage to be their best self.

As Nadya fell headfirst to the ground, time slowed down. It always does in such moments of heightened urgency or intensity. Adrenaline floods our system, giving us acute awareness of events.

Many of the cast watched on a monitor backstage, either at the edge of the bench seat gulfed in fear, or in the middle of an extreme stretch on the backstage tent floor.

Her head was on a very direct course to the ground. At each passing moment, we're collectively thinking, #OMG, Nadya is going to die. Five less feet to go. #$@& what about her kids? The next five feet vanish. She's going to break her neck! No!

Death or serious injury is not front of mind; however, we are all aware of the risk. We all understand the value of knowing our colleagues are looking out for us. We must trust. We must be confident that team members care enough to put our safety first when needed.

Off to the side of this powerful human tower is a fellow Russian acrobat. His name is Konstantin. In this specific moment in the act, he plays the role of, spotter. His job is to protect (spot) Nadya if she is in danger. Question is, has time run out. Will his female comrade break her neck on his watch?

———

Chapter 3
Impactful Discovery

It wasn't until my late forties that I discovered the incredible power and true value of empathy on a personal level. I had grasped its concept on the Cirque du Soleil stage, but I had no idea that so many people lacked what if offered. Empathy is about feeling cared for, protected, seen, heard and understood... SAFE.

I hadn't yet learned that so many people felt alone, lonely, and disconnected.

I too have had phases of isolation, disconnectedness and loneliness. On the outside, I appeared vibrant and optimistic, which I am most times. However, on the inside, I cried, fraught for understanding. I craved connection and a sense of belonging.

There are too many who experience deficits in meaningful connection and emotional security. As a result, they emotionally calcify. They hide their feelings in dark, silent corners. Or they wear masks, feigning happiness and fulfillment to experience a sense of belonging and validation... because being positive is cool and attractive.

If you are not feeling any form of emotional deficit, or have not experienced that empty feeling, it's highly probable that somebody you care for deeply is. They are going through something painful, and you have no idea. It could be your best friend, your son or daughter, your husband/wife or significant other, your mother, uncle, or a colleague you think you know. They desperately wish you knew what plagues their soul. They desperately want to be vulnerable and share. They desperately want to feel safe, be seen, heard, and understood. They anxiously need you to be there with them. Note the careful word selection... be there WITH them, not FOR them.

Brother Christian had walked WITH Matthew McConaughey for over three hours in the desert. His two defining words were the epitome of empathy. He had listened void of judgment. He had listened void of advice. He had listened void of motivation.

His simple and effective response to Matthew's troubled journey of confusion and temptation was simply, "Me, too."

There is no one-size-fits-all way to express empathy. This was Brother Michael's sincere and authentic way.

———

PINK IS THE COLOR OF EMPATHY
Becoming a high-value person in a disconnected world

Chapter 4
Empathy Sounds Like

The below list will help you understand what empathy sounds like. By using the structure and intention of the sentences whenever somebody you care about is going through a hard time, this could be depression or other emotional crises, you will develop the ability to better support and understand them, let alone develop deeper bonds--deeper intimacy.

If you, yourself are going through a crisis, these tools will help you better gauge your emotional needs. It will give you the ability to communicate those needs. Communication is after all the foundation of all healthy or unhealthy relationships. It's a combination of what we say, when we say it and how we say it.

In future chapters we will address how to recover from crisis, including mental and emotional health situations. It's good to understand and learn both sides of the equation.

1. Me too.
2. That makes total sense.
3. That would have hurt my feelings too.
4. You're in a tough spot.
5. What I admire most about what you're doing is...
6. I get that.
7. I'd feel the same way if that happened to me.
8. What do you see as your options?
9. That sounds horrible.
10. I wish you didn't have to go through that.
11. I'm on your side.
12. I wish I could have been with you in that moment.
13. I support your position.
14. I would have trouble coping with that.
15. No wonder you're upset/frustrated/disappointed.
16. I'd feel the same way you do in your situation.
17. It would be great to be free of this.
18. That would make me mad too.
19. That would make me sad too.
20. That must have annoyed you.
21. Wow, that must have hurt.
22. That would make me feel insecure.
23. That sounds a little frightening.

These are examples of effective phrases that will help you communicate your empathy if you are wanting to be supportive and understanding. I don't recommend using them verbatim. Doing so could make them sound robotic and insincere and, therefore, defeat the purpose. Leverage them as examples or guidelines. Make them your own, expressed in your own voice, and in your own way.

Another effective strategy is to ask open-ended questions. This invites them to share more. Your invitation to elaborate communicates that you are curious, which means you care. In the book *The Coaching Habit*, by Michael Bungay Stanier, he talks about his concept in great depth. Talk less, he says. Ask open-ended questions that allow them to go anywhere they want to. That makes it all about them, which is empathy at its finest.

Examples of great open-ended question to show you are curious and care:

"Tell me what's on your mind?" Then let them talk and talk and talk. Just listen to understand. When they stop talking, you could go ever deeper by asking, "What else?" This process is permission and encouragement to share, share, share, while you listen, listen, listen. This approach is incredibly healing for that person, making you a high-value person. Listening void of judgment heals!

Make sure you mean and feel what you say and ask. Use the impactful H.A.I.L. acronym, which I'll break down in a future chapter.

As with all things, "Practice doesn't make perfect. Practice makes permanent." Thanks for that insight, Vince Lombardi.

Enjoy the difference such phrases will make in your relationships. Use them intentionally and take note on how people respond to you. I'm confident you will witness a positive difference in your relationships.

You're welcome.

———

Chapter 5

This Is What Empathy Doesn't Sound Like

THIS IS NOT PINK When something terrible happens to a friend or loved one, it can be difficult to know what to say.

That's why we often reach for one of these common responses, that was compiled in a blog by Laura Click, titled, *31 Empathetic Statements for When You Don't Know What to Say:*

https://medium.com/@lauraclick/31-empathetic-statements-for-when-you-dont-know-what-to-say-edd50822c96a

> "Everything happens for a reason."
> "This too shall pass."
> "Just look on the bright side…"
> "God has a plan."
> "I know how you feel."
> "He's in a better place now."
> "This could be a blessing in disguise."
> "Something better is around the corner."

Although these statements sound good in theory, they rarely do much to help the other person feel better. Instead, it often minimizes the other person's pain or discomfort, doing little to connect with how he, she, they are feeling. The disconnect comes from the apparent insensitivity or lack of understanding of their situation.

Having empathy is one thing. Being able to effectively communicate it so it is clearly received, understood, and felt is another.

With all that I have shared so far, please keep in mind that there is no exact right and wrong, only styles and strategies that optimize the outcome of any given situation. In other words, empathy is neither a one-size fits all, nor is it mandatory in every circumstance. Adapt to the situation and the person.

Whichever love language you may use, motivation or empathy, it will be based on how well you know that person and understand their needs. Sometimes, a cold, insensitive, motivational kick up the bum may be what the doctor ordered. Know your friends. Know thyself: Emotional Intelligence.

Please revert to these two chapters often, as we all need reminders.

**Self-awareness is the
first step to change anything.**

Now that you've read the "what empathy doesn't sound like" list, ask yourself the following questions, and be very bold and honest with your answers… nobody needs to know other than you.

1. Are you the type of person who likes to motivate people and play cheerleader? If so, step back at each individual situation (and person), asking yourself, is it motivation they need right now or a lending ear? Adjust accordingly and observe if there is any difference for the other person.
2. Are you more inclined to simply listen and not offer advice or motivation? Step back and evaluate if the person's need or desire is empathy, motivation or a kick up the bum.

Chapter 6
Foundations

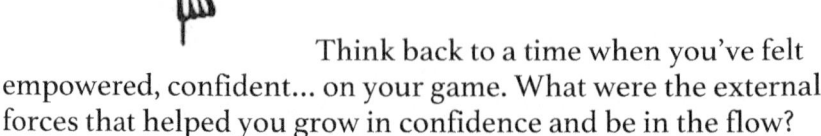

Think back to a time when you've felt empowered, confident... on your game. What were the external forces that helped you grow in confidence and be in the flow?

Usually, the forces of self-confidence are established and built during childhood. When healthy supportive parents or guardians feel the pain of their child, they instinctually sooth, nurture and reassure. They are there for and with the child. When children experience setbacks, all it takes is a warm loving set of parental arms wrapped around them to put the world back together again. Such warmth enables children to feel seen, heard, and understood... safe... loved.

Well, the same human responses are present in our teenage years and as adults. This feeling of safety and love can only be provided through caring and understanding. It requires another human protecting your wellbeing and honoring the essence of who you are... and who you are not.

Hopefully, your parents were there for you. You were surrounded and fueled by love, support, understood and encouraged. Your emotional, spiritual, and mental needs were met. You were never made to feel irrelevant. Your emotional, spiritual, and mental bank account was solid. This healthy stable foundation set you up for a promising and wealthy future.

Even with such a healthy childhood, children experience scars or trauma whenever the world denies their existence in any capacity: at school, from teachers, classmates, and so forth. We are social beings and therefore need community. Even the most extreme introverts need community. The size of the village is relative.

At the opposite end of the emotional spectrum, the neglected child, the misunderstood child, the invisible child, the traumatized child will face a seemingly insurmountable uphill battle. It will be difficult to grow wings, let alone fly without a net. It won't be impossible, just difficult.

Without empathy, a parent can't be a good parent. They will be incapable of validating their child's emotions. This will cause a profound emotive void that the child will struggle to fill for the remainder of their life. That child will not have a launching pad from which to fly. Over time if left unresolved, the void will become a highly detrimental and self-sabotaging mental health issue.

Unfortunately, the pace of modern society has promoted an emotional void for kids. It concerns me who and what our children will become. I don't mean this in the sense of, "back in the day things were better," but rather that technology has brought about a change that the human brain is having trouble adapting to. Luckily, children are resilient and will adapt. Societal growth pains will leave deep scars, and trauma, nonetheless. We are already seeing the impact.

Without empathy, a friend can't be a good friend. Without empathy, a romantic partner can't be a great partner.

Life without experiencing empathy is painful and lonely on any level: at home with a disconnected and indifferent loved one, at work with a heartless boss, and among our fake friends who undermine us behind our backs.

Regarding the heartless boss, even though this is not a book about leadership, we can't deny the impact of working with a bad boss. Most people spend more time at work with that boss than with family and friends (until COVID).

That bad boss simply hadn't taken the time to understand or see YOU. They lacked respect. The lacked appreciation. Because they were indifferent and potentially arrogant assholes (or extremely insecure), they may not have even felt guilt or remorse for treating you badly. Working with a bad boss sucks. In fact, people usually quit a bad boss over their actual job. I hope you have never had that type of boss, though the odds that you have at some point, are high. If you have, send me the name and address of your worst boss ever. I know a guy who knows a guy with zero empathy.

According to studies by groups like Gallup and DDI there is a direct correlation between bad bosses and employee turnover. Development Dimensions International (DDI) collected data regarding more than a one thousand managers and senior leaders. Employees experience high levels of stress and anxiety. The financial math is simple. It costs companies billions of dollars.

Yet, the majority stay silent about their negative, even toxic experiences.

**Even the toughest amongst us,
the stoics, the heartless, the
independent souls need
empathy from somebody.**

Chapter 7
Ignite

Why do people stay silent when struggling? Why do you, or why have you protected your vulnerability? How do we not see the needs of others? Why have others not felt or understood your pain when you were struggling? The thing is, we can't control what we feel. All we can do is manage our responses to those feelings. But as emotional beings, how and what we feel drives decisions and behaviors, including how we view and treat others.

Humans are motivated by two things. We either, run away from pain, or we run toward pleasure. Both emotions inspire action. The harder you feel, the more you'll be compelled to act.

PINK IS THE COLOR OF EMPATHY

Becoming a high-value person in a disconnected world

If you experience something extremely joyful and pleasurable, the odds are high that you will desire that same euphoria again. As a result, you'll do something. In fact, many become addicted to the intense release of feel-good hormones or neurotransmitters such as:

- serotonin (mood stabilizer)
- dopamine (happy/reward hormone)
- oxytocin (bonding, love, trust)
- endorphins (pain relief, runners high)

And let's not forget the impact of an appetizing dose of delectable chocolate that stimulates the release of phenylethylamine (the in-love hormone).

Such hormones can inspire addiction... which is an intense desire or need to experience something again, and again... compulsion.

In stark contrast, if you experience something that causes you so much pain and suffering, you will either fawn or freeze... or, be compelled to action (fight).

When it comes to pain, unless we have experienced profound pain or loss, and processed it by allowing ourselves to fully experience it, we are commonly unable to see it in others. We are uninspired or lack motivation to take action or help, let alone understand. Case in point, a friend of mine sadly lost her daughter to leukemia. As a result, she created a leukemia foundation. Her pain turned to purpose. But she needed to experience and feel that pain to truly understand it. Understanding is one step. Taking action is another, nonetheless.

Her suffering ignited a drive to become more than she was. Her pain turned her into a high-value person, providing priceless resources to those who are directly or indirectly impacted by cancer. Empathy inspires action. It fuels change for the betterment of human life.

Cancer was once upon a time such a taboo topic. Through awareness and understanding people can now openly talk about it. The stigma has been removed. Those with cancer have been set free to share their diagnosis void of shame. Awareness has provided a safe and supportive network filled with understanding and compassion.

Because most of us know somebody who is fighting, or somebody who has died of cancer, it becomes easy to empathize with the devastation of the disease. Think of how many souls are comforted with this collective empathy.

Now imagine that YOU have cancer or a toxic boss, boyfriend/girlfriend/husband/wife and people feel WITH you. How powerful and beautiful. How comforting and reassuring.

At the opposite end of the spectrum, you share your emotional struggles or clinical diagnosis (depression, anxiety and other disorders) and people begin talking about themselves, or start to avoid you.

"Oh, a friend of mine had cancer once. She survived it after two years of chemo. She's now living happily up in Main. She has this awesome dog, Tennison" ... Blah blah blah.

OR

They become "motivational speakers' to help you along in your suffering.

"Dude, bro... with modern medical practices, I wouldn't worry. They cure cancer all the time, now. Stop stressing out about it "

Easy for you to say. You don't have cancer. And if you did, I'm sure you'd be a little concerned.

PINK IS THE COLOR OF EMPATHY

Becoming a high-value person in a disconnected world

Both these behaviors are incredibly common and fueled by good intentions. Both these behaviors provide little value to a person in emotional need. Feel with them first and you will be of high value. Because that's what empathy does.

Life is filled with surprises, irony, contradictions, unknowns, and confusions. And when it happens to us, we often become the center of the universe in our pain. Yet to others, who fail to empathize, lack of understanding or indifference is the painful response. We are left feeling alone and disconnected, with our tragedy undermined. All the while, social media is reminding us how great everybody else's life is. This magnifies the disconnect and aloneness.

How easy is it to not grasp the concept of starvation when it's happening on the other side of the world? If people are dying on the other side of the world (or the country), news headlines may inspire a moment of sympathy, but it's not enough. We have become desensitized due to overexposure to bad news on television and social media. It's all just a swipe away. This is no critic on human behavior. It's perfectly normal and understandable.

When it comes to more common emotional setbacks like heartbreak, which we all experience at some point, it's easy to forget how paralyzing and debilitating it was before we moved on and had fully healed or found new love. However, when we are in the thick of a painful separation or divorce, we crave a lending ear, we desire a warm comforting heart to help carry the pain... we want and need empathy. We all want and need empathy. If only we could all reciprocate to the same degree we want and need it gifted to us.

Empathy is particularly beautiful when humanity shares it collectively. It inspires togetherness and denies differences. As a result, humans become angels, providing help, resources, and assistance to those in need: earthquakes for example, or flooding and other natural disasters.

Our pain and suffering awakens something, compelling us to act and become proactive. Sadly, unmanaged pain can have the complete opposite effect. It can turn us into cold, heartless beings that inflict pain and suffering on others. Life is full of choices. I hope that empathy becomes one of yours because empathy changes lives. Empathy saves lives.

When empathy is properly understood and effectively shared or leveraged, it changes everything in our lives for the better. There are, however, necessary terms and conditions to optimize its power.

Throughout these pages we will explore and reveal the deeper meaning, and maybe more importantly, how you can leverage empathy to your gain.

Here's the catch!

Empathy is considered a benevolent art form. It can also be lent to the practice of the dark arts. In fact, "the dark empath" (a person with heightened gifts of empathy) is considered to be the most dangerous personality types. They exhibit similar behavioral traits as the narcissist. The difference being that the narcissist has zero empathy... so they say. We'll explore this common belief in more depth later.

Did you know that FBI agents use empathy during interrogations? It's called "Tactical Empathy." We'll talk about this in depth, just in case you're ever being interrogated, you'll know what to expect.

Like every human trait and human invention, the intention with which it's applied determines benevolence or malevolence.

How you choose to use the information in this book is up to you. I'm writing, nonetheless, to ignite goodness, inspire healthy connection, prosperous romance, deeper friendships, better communication, and overall elevated emotional intelligence. The lessons also apply to sales, entrepreneurship, and leadership.

Empathy is a skill like any other human skill. If you get a chance to practice, you can get better at it.

Simon Baron Cohen

Chapter 8
The Sob Story

I've talked about workplace trauma, adult relationship trauma and childhood and trauma. Humans (in particular, parents) lack emotional intelligence and decent parenting skills. Most seeds of adult trauma are rooted in the emotional wounds that happen to us during childhood. Too often, we ignore or deny those wounds as adults. They manifest and get stronger, if and when, left unchecked.

Hurt people, hurt people.

In many ways I lived as a stoic teen and adult, denying my traumatic childhood.

By the time we reach adulthood, we have developed coping strategies to mask the pain. Some choose highly destructive means that become addictions to soothe. Some choose fun, shiny distractions. Others overachieve to compensate. I am not casting judgment on the way in which people navigate their lives. I am acknowledging what I have observed and learned.

Ambition, hope and imagination had been my distractions. Until....

Hello darkness my old friend. I've come to talk with you again.

Yes, you may recognize those lyrics from the Simon and Garfunkel classic, "The Sound of Silence." Silence had become a deafening cancer during my mid to late forties. Isolation, guilt, and tainted shadows were my companions. Hopelessness, my new norm. Like too many humans, I felt alone and lonely.

Our wounds and darkness will always find us if left unchecked. Without being processed, the hurt, anger, and pain of life manifests. They brew. They ferment. How do I know? Because one day my system could no longer prevent the spewing of a toxic and desperate state of mind. Depression. Mental illness.

I wish they could understand me. I wish I could share it.

I experienced my first major depression while performing in Cirque du Soleil's *Mystère*. Despite the great achievement and the semblance of success, emptiness and loneliness nullified the amazing gravity-defying feat. Achievement always comes at a cost or sacrifice. Beware of what you are giving up while pursuing your carrot. Success as in the typical interpretation of the word, money, power, and status is shallow and fleeting. Without love and connection, human existence is empty and painful. Love and connection are the emotional fuels that drive and promote fulfillment – that is true wealth – if you have your health, too.

My lack of emotional fuel was born from a traumatic childhood. At least that's what most psychologists will tell you… a cliché

diagnosis or judgment. Kind of like what judgmental street psychologist will conclude about the dude buying an extravagant sports car to compensate for his small…
Sometimes it's true. Sometimes it's not. Know thyself.

I believe my trauma was and is real. In many ways, I fit the standard psychological narrative of an abused child. The consequences of not addressing my trauma became painfully apparent in my late twenties. A denied and prolonged emotional health issue turned into a mental health issue.

One of many solutions to help deny childhood trauma is to become an over-achiever or to choose a career that brings public acclaim. I chose the performing arts, the stage. I ran away with the circus. But not just any circus. *Mesdames et messieurs, Le Cirque du Soleil.* I became addicted to the applause, the prestige and the respect and admiration that was afforded me.

My brain translated the applause as love, acceptance and belonging. The theatrical stage provided me a haven that humans had failed to provide. Everything comes at a cost, including success and achievement.

In pursuing the American dream, I diluted all ties from my family in Belgium and England. The existing bonds were weak and easy to break. They were bonds, nonetheless. Perhaps the only ones I knew.

I moved to New York at the age of twenty-eight, never looking back. A desire to live a dream or achieve a goal is unto itself not a bad thing. It's only detrimental when the subconscious motivation is not purely for the love of doing that thing, but rather the addiction to the rewards the achievement provides. In other words, the sense of purpose was internal and materialistic, or selfish even, despite finding great joy in sharing my passion and talent with the Cirque audience. Touching the hearts and souls of mesmerized audiences was an honor. But at twenty-eight, I was still too self-absorbed, lacking emotional intelligence. It was still too much about me.

One of the many benefits of taking time out to understand the person in the mirror is that it invites and enables empathy for the self. We don't self-soothe enough. In fact, many ambitious people are very hard on themselves to meet their own high standards. Then there are the perfectionists who can take ambition and expectation to toxic levels with never a moment of self-empathy.

Adding to the value of self-awareness is understanding that pain and trauma often lead people to the arts to mask and manage their psychosis. I was not a freak after all, even though I felt like one. The healthy aspect of the arts is the therapeutic nature of expression. It helps calm the soul and exorcise demons.

So, what traumatic event happened to me in childhood that unfortunately happens to way too many young souls?

Once upon a time in 1967 when I was three and living in London, my father was arrested for abuse. I and my two half-brothers, Jean-Pierre, and Rudy were his prey. He allegedly served some time for his crimes.

My mother couldn't' handle the reality of his actions and found salvation in the company of Guinness and gin – Mom became an alcoholic. She would often throw my brothers and me out onto the cold wet winter streets of London during her moments of drunken anger and dysfunction. We slept in doorways to fight the cold. Stole food to eat out of desperation. We, essentially, lived on the streets.

At the age of seven the British authorities placed me and my brothers into childcare – a home similar to an orphanage. There were drugs, regular fistfights, stabbings, teenage prostitution, even attempted suicides.

Through it all, I observed my brothers. They remained, strong, courageous, hopeful, and full of belief that we'd be okay. My eldest brother Jean-Pierre would always say, "Stay positive, Vital. Use Will Power to overcome. Use will power to not be afraid. Use Will Power to make the pain go away. Use Will Power to make the cold disappear. Stay positive and believe it's all gonna be okay."

They gave me strength and inspired me to always believe, to always have an optimistic attitude. I've since relied on that mindset to keep me alive, to keep me moving forward even when the chips were down as a teen. I've used the power of attitude as an adult while pursuing my dreams, hungry to make them come true, but also, to become a better human being, both at home and at work.

Along the journey of life, we are presented with endless forks in the road. We make decisions. We choose what type of person we are. We choose integrity, or not. We choose love or hate. We choose empathy or not. I hope you choose all the positives, in particular empathy.

During my childhood, I had many role models. Some direct and intentional, others by proximity. Those that chose to share love and empathy with me, were an integral part of me not going down dark paths and not dying before the age of eighteen. Statistics had predicted that I'd be dead or in jail by the age of eighteen due to gang related violence, drugs, or suicide.

The sudden passing of my mom when I was sixteen, who lived in Belgium, provided an opportunity to be reunited with my Belgian father. At first it was magical. But with ties cut off from the English foster care system, the narcissist pedophile soon emerged. It's not a Disney story. You can read the full version in my top-selling book, *FLYING WITHOUT A NET*. It's a different type of circus than Cirque du Soleil (despite performing in two of their shows for over five years).

The success of performing in the world's most prestigious and renowned modern circus was an ego booster. "I had made it."

BUT!

The thing about success is that it's empty when you have nobody to share it with. The initial high is addictive, nonetheless. But when you are home alone at night, the loneliness looms like an approaching hurricane.

To add to the emptiness, I couldn't share my despair. I feared judgment. I feared losing friendships. I lived in a heightened sense of fight or flight. This mindset didn't make sense!

How can I be living my dream yet feeling so broken?

Here's why. Without human connection, love and empathy, life is worthless and meaningless. Meaning is powerful. Purpose is wealth, but without meaning, it lacks a compass. I highly recommend reading Victor Frankl's, *Man's Search for Meaning*. It tells the tale of how and why some Jews emotionally survived the Holocaust, while others gave up and died of "natural causes."

I now know that I am not alone in my depression and fear. I now know that so many, too many, live with anxiety, depression and loneliness.

By my late forties, the depression had reached new lows. Thoughts and visions of suicide crossed my mind. For me, suicide was not about wanting to die. It was a question of not knowing how to live another day with such suffering. I never wanted to die.

I believe that extended emotional trauma turns to poor mental health when left unchecked. Yet, mental health practitioners treat the symptoms the same way. Some do have mental disorders, and some have emotional disorders. Are they the same? I don't think so and should, therefore, be treated and categorized differently.

Though mental and emotional health can be defined differently, multiple qualities separate them from each other. For one, mental and emotional health process different parts of your mind and conduct. The state of your mental health reflects how well your mind processes information and experiences. On the other hand, your emotional health revolves around how you express your emotions based on those experiences. In a sense, your mental and emotional health handle especially different parts of your mind.

Emotional health encompasses more than just the state of your feelings. Rather, emotional health involves your ability to manage and express your emotions in a mature and appropriate manner.

DiscoveryPlace.info

Chapter 9

Premature Goodbyes

There have been multiple times when I've been connected to somebody who ended their life by suicide. It's painful. It evokes intense feelings of guilt and helplessness. Perhaps you have also lost a loved one to suicide and can relate to the pain of grieving their choice and your inability to help or save them? Hopefully you haven't. If you have, know that you are not alone.

My first encounter was back in England while living in the institution. I was about thirteen or fourteen. One of the girls in the home, Debbie, mixed race, had gotten caught up in drugs and prostitution before she had even turned fifteen. She shared her secret adventures with me, some in graphic detail. They were as much entertaining as they were tragic and gruesome for a young teenage boy who still found girls disgusting.

She had warned me that she wanted to run away from the home, as many kids did or wanted to, including me. Debbie shared how much she hated her life and the world. "I sometimes wish I would fall asleep one day and never wake up," she said, sucking hard on the last puffs of her cigarette.

I listened, thinking it was an empty threat coming from the mouth of a dysfunctional and rebellious teen desperate for attention-- desperate for a sense of love, belonging and security--empathy.

As promised, Debbie ran away. We never saw or heard from her again. I can't confirm it, but rumor says she died of an overdose. She had taken her life. I could only hope it was painless and that her soul found peace.

As young and inexperienced as I was, a part of me questioned if I could have done something to help her. Could I have listened more or longer? Should I have believed her cries for help? Though I logically understand that I was indeed too young, I still feel regret and guilt to this day.

I have friends and family who have lost daughters, siblings, or significant others to suicide. I don't want to even begin to imagine the levels of pain, loss, guilt and regret they may feel.

My most painful and most guilt-evoking incident came when I was in my late forties. A female friend had recently broken up with what she said was the love of her life. I spent a Thursday evening with her. From about 7:00 p.m. to 1:00 a.m., I listened and did my best to distract her. When I dropped her off at their house, (they still lived together), she asked me to stay and talk more. I was emotionally exhausted from listening.

"Just another ten minutes?" she asked. "I'm not ready to go inside."

"I'll text you first thing in the morning. I'll pick you up for lunch," I said.

"Thank you. I love you," she replied.

She gave me a big, long, and powerful hug. I watched her walk to her front door. It was evident she was dejected. She disappeared into the house.

She never responded to my morning texts. My phone calls remained unreturned. At about four o'clock that Friday afternoon, I was informed she had died of suicide. A sheet around her neck, apparently. I cried and cried. I cried and cried for her mom. I cried for her. I cried for me. No parent should lose a child. I cried some more. Eyes swollen with guilt and remorse, I hid in solitude for days.

How could you have been so insensitive, Vital?
How did you not see all the signs?
Why didn't she just tell me?
Why didn't she ask for help?

The thing is, she did ask. She did tell me in the way she could. I wasn't listening. I wasn't really listening.

Listening is an art form and a heavily undermined part of communication. We usually tend to focus on the delivery of a message rather than how we receive a message.

There are five pillars to listening. We will address them in depth later in the book.

Chapter 10
Courage and Cowards

It must take incredible courage and vulnerability to declare that one's soul is so hurt and/or broken that suicide appears to be the only and best option to be free of the suffering.

One of the most common responses after the suicide is, "Why didn't they say something?"

"If they had only told me. I would have been there for them. If only they had said something."

It is so easy to say that after the fact. Why don't we communicate our love and support more often? Why don't we do so when people are actually still alive? It's a strange and disconnected form of communication that we only share how we really loved and valued a person when it's too late--at their funeral.

So why don't broken souls, the depressed, and the suicidal just simply ask? Why don't they just say something? I think this is the wrong question. Why do we put the responsibility on a soul that is obviously compromised to carry the burden of being so vulnerable and simply telling us how they feel, when our world tells us it's not safe to do so?

I can only speak from experience, along with a heavy dose of personal research and in-depth conversations with those connected to suicide.

Once upon a time, I had held a box cutter inches from my wrist while lying in my bathtub. I had lost hope. I didn't want to die; I no longer had the emotional fortitude to continue. I took a deep breath and yelled. I yelled and placed the box cutter up against my wrist.

I'm so scared.
So lost.
So confused.
So alone.
So empty.
Somebody please help me.
God?
Screw you dude!
Why would you begin listening now? Why would I start believing in you again? When did prayers ever make a difference? If they did, surely there would be less suffering on this plane of existence and consciousness.

It's been said that suicide is the most cowardly and selfish of acts a human can do. One goes straight to hell for committing the consummate sin. The very word "commit" says it all. You commit a crime. You commit adultery. You commit murder... and then you commit suicide. You are a criminal. You've done a really bad and selfish thing. You should be ashamed of yourself!

I was ashamed of myself. Everything I had ever learned and observed about life told me I was a dirty, negative, selfish, and shameful coward. So many people who are dying due to health reasons would die to live. And here I was, numbed by the miracle of life, indifferent, ungrateful.

Society would judge and condemn me. I'd be banished to hell. Yet, self-inflicted death was easier to face than my peers. If hell exists, then experiencing hell on earth is the ultimate motivation behind ending one's life... committing suicide.

With the pressure of the sharp blade indented in my skin, I felt a deep, dark, and unknown level of fear. My determination to end the suffering combatted that fear. The need for an end of suffering won.

My breathing became heavy, heartbeat pulsing as if on crack. I cried like I hadn't in... well, forever. I didn't want to die. I just wanted to end the chronic and relentless torture.

I don't want to die.
Please, give me the strength to face life or end it.

My dead mom's photo sat on the edge of the bathtub. I was so afraid to see her again prematurely. Would she judge me, too?

I'm sorry mom. I've let you down. Please don't hate me.

I had tried hard to share my pain with a few very close friends over the course of the past months. Some cared in the way they could with me only sharing a fraction of the story. Some of them slowly created distance.
I get it.

Who wants to hang out with a person who is negative or lacks gratitude? Who wants to be around such dark, heavy, and oxygen-sucking energy?

My friends and family won't understand.
Why can't they simply understand me?

I've read multiple times that it is impossible to be in a state of gratitude and sadness at the same time. Gratitude leads to happiness they say. Ouch!

You ungrateful bastard, Vital.

Burning daggers of shame and condemnation pierced my back. Arrows punctured my once stoic heart. I am not alone in my shame and guilt. Someone you love is feeling the same thing right now.

My friends and family won't understand.
Why can't they simply understand me?
Why?

Society makes suicide so, so shameful. How selfish of us to want somebody to keep living in a state of suffering. It's selfish because WE don't want them to die. We don't want to morn. It's not about me or you, it's about the person suffering. If you love and care for somebody, why would you want to prolong their suffering. Why wouldn't we help them to end the unfathomable pain in a dignified manner where they can transition surrounded by love and understanding, rather than alone and in a state of pain and desperation. I subscribe to Dr. Kevorkian's philosophy of assisted suicide where the process is as painless as possible and in an environment that is gentle and safe.

Having said that, I don't want anybody to kill themselves. I would hope to save them, but only through love and empathy which will hopefully INSPIRE them to live another day rather than guilting them into another minute of emotional torture on this plain of existence. Surely that is compassion and humane? I want to save lives by inspiring them not guilting them.

Why are we so selfish?
Why did could nobody understand me?

Why did I slit my wrists?

Some people are just not meant to be in this world.

Phoebe Stone
The Boy on Cinnamon Street

PINK IS THE COLOR OF EMPATHY

Becoming a high-value person in a disconnected world

As you read this, ask yourself the following questions, and be very bold and honest with your answers... nobody needs to know other than you.

1. Were you judging me in any way shape or form for wanting to die of suicide?
2. Were you feeling sympathy?
3. Were you feeling pity?
4. Anger?
5. Were you indifferent?
6. Would you like to give me a hug?
7. Were you wondering why I hadn't really asked for help?

Chapter 11
Sad Stats

At the time of my darkest chapter, I was oblivious as to the amount of people who contemplated, attempted, or completed suicide. You too may be surprised.

Here are some suicide stats according to the CDC:

- o Suicide rates increased 30% between 2000–2018 and declined in 2019 and 2020.
- o Suicide is a leading cause of death in the United States, with 45,979 deaths in 2020. This is about one death every 11 minutes. The number of people who think about or attempt suicide is even higher.

- In 2020, an estimated 12.2 million American adults seriously thought about suicide, 3.2 million planned a suicide attempt, and 1.2 million attempted suicides.
- Suicide affects all ages. In 2020, suicide was among the top 9 leading causes of death for people ages 10-64. Suicide was the second leading cause of death for people ages 10-14 and 25-34.

I had become a statistic.

I don't want to die.
I can't carry on!
Please, somebody help me.
I don't want to become a statistic.

According to the United Health Foundation:

Risk factors associated with suicide among adolescents include:

- Psychiatric disorders such as major depressive, bipolar, substance use and conduct disorders.
- Psychiatric comorbidity, especially the combination of mood, disruptive and substance abuse disorders.
- Family history of depression or suicide.
- Loss of a parent to death or divorce.
- Physical and/or sexual abuse.
- Lack of a support network.
- Feelings of social isolation.
- Bullying.

The teen suicide rate is higher among:

- Males than females. However, females have more attempts compared with males.
- American Indian/Alaska Native adolescents compared to other race/ethnicity groups. White adolescents have a higher teen suicide rate compared with Asian/Pacific

Islander adolescents, Hispanic adolescents, and Black adolescents.
- Suicide attempts are higher among students who identified as gay, lesbian or bisexual compared with students who identified as heterosexual.

The cost of suicide attempts in the United States in 2019 was estimated to be $70 billion. And please remember, somebody in your direct or indirect circle is contemplating suicide. They may need you more than you'll ever know, in particular if you have teens somewhere in your life.

https://www.americashealthrankings.org/explore/health-of-women-and-children/measure/teen_suicide/state/ALL

PINK IS THE COLOR OF EMPATHY

Becoming a high-value person in a disconnected world

Empathy saves lives

Chapter 12
Spocibo

I once thought I might die during my five years in Cirque du Soleil due to human error. Those type of thoughts are back of mind, but they happen. The company does the best it can to minimize injury, let alone death. Nonetheless, things get overlooked… until they happen.

During my bungee trapeze act in *Mystère,* my colleague forgot to tie-off my bungee cords. They would normally be secured to a structure as I flew forty-five feet above the audience. I remember falling longer toward the audience… longer than normal, thinking, "It had been a good run and that today is when it ended." I embraced death. Suddenly, I felt the bungee cords tighten. It wasn't a good day to die. Luckily, Cirque had installed a back-up measure with the end of my cords being fixed permanently to the tech grid. Thank you, *merci* and *dank u wel*. *Spocibo* (spu'si'bo) in Russian.

Which brings me back to Nadya. With time and space running out, would she die, break her neck or be saved by Konstantin, her spotter.

Konstantin had a fraction of a second to act. What did he do?

He accelerated like a turbo rocket, running toward Nadya. He did a baseball-like slide into home plate. He got in-between Nadya and the ground, breaking his leg to save the ninety-five-pound falling angel in white. Yes! Konstantin broke his leg in the process of saving Nadya.

Without the element of caring, there is no way Cirque performers go out and risk their lives to entertain the millions of eyes that experience the marvel of the companies' genius experiences. Without the element of caring watching protectively from the wings, there is no way anybody in this environment risks anything in order to reach higher or fly without a net.

Knowing that somebody cares and has your back, empowers. It spurs confidence and promotes trust, making you a high-value person. If you can't trust somebody, they have little emotional value and the connection will only be superficial.

That healthy journey of love, nurture and security should begin in childhood. It is easier to raise healthy children than to fix broken adults.

―――――――

That healthy journey of love, nurture and security should begin in childhood. It is easier to raise healthy children than to fix broken adults.

PINK IS THE COLOR OF EMPATHY

Becoming a high-value person in a disconnected world

Some dreams are so lifelike.

Chapter 13
Nightmare

I opened my eyes in shock. I was alive, breathing and feeling. Some dreams are so lifelike.

What kind of messed up nightmare was that? I hadn't "committed" suicide.

I didn't commit an alleged crime. I don't need to feel dirty and guilty... my soul isn't going to hell! More importantly, I'm not a coward or that selfish. Too many think that suicide is cloaked in an endless list of negative characteristics.

Most people who die of suicide have been incredibly strong and courageous for years! As I make this bold statement, I am aware that each situation is unique and that my comments are a generalization. There are always exceptions in life and death. There is no "one-size-fits-all." Nonetheless, I think it unfair to label suicide as a generally weak or cowardly act. It is far from cowardly. It is far from a crime. It is not selfish. It is not a sin.

The real crime is lacking empathy and condemning their choices. Lacking empathy is a sin. I wish society judged, condemned, and shamed those lacking empathy as much as they condemn the suicidal, the different, and the social rebels who challenge the status quo and hold mirrors up to reflect how ugly we can be as a species.

Did I just say that out loud?

YEP! I did. I'll say it again if need be.

If you lack empathy, I condemn thee to burn in eternal indifference and aimlessly float in a black hole without an ounce of empathy, compassion, or respect in return. No love. No connection. No sense of belonging. No purpose... and even less meaning. The ultimate emotional void. The ultimate torture. Infinite isolation and invisibility. You may as well exist without a soul, tempted to commit suicide to escape the unfathomable torment.

I'm not a religious man, but this is a good time to channel Ezekiel 25:17 while leveraging my inner Samuel L. Jackson (*Pulp Fiction* monologue).

... The path of the righteous man is beset on all sides
By the inequities of the selfish and the tyranny of evil men
Blessed is he who, in the name of charity and good will

Shepherds the weak through the valley of darkness
For he is truly his brother's keeper and the finder of lost children
And I will strike down upon thee
With great vengeance and furious anger
Those who attempt to poison and destroy my brothers
And you will know my name is the Lord
When I lay my vengeance upon thee

I hated those heartless people who didn't care. I hated this planet for its greed and ugliness, for the suffering and violation of human rights. Why couldn't people allow gays to marry? Why are transgenders so misunderstood and feared? Why so much ugliness and hate?

Why do they wish to ban certain books and deny history be told truthfully, even if it's ugly and shameful?

I genuinely don't understand humankind.

Why have women been suppressed and violated for so long? Why were slaves whipped, sodomized, castrated, raped, and stripped of their history, home, and identity? Why? Why were six million Jews sent to premature deaths? Why does man go to war? Why? Why? Why? Why was half of the Belgian Congolese population mutilated and murdered for rubber? Why? Help it make sense.

I genuinely don't understand humankind. I totally relate to John Coffey in the movie, *The Green Mile,* played by Michael Clarke.

"I'm tired boss.

Tired of bein' on the road, lonely as a sparrow in the rain. Tired of not ever having me a buddy to be with, or tell me where we's coming from or going to, or why. Mostly I'm tired of people being ugly to each other. I'm tired of all the pain I feel and hear in the world every day." – The Green Mile.

Why?

PINK IS THE COLOR OF EMPATHY

Becoming a high-value person in a disconnected world

Because of a lack of empathy, that's why.

It becomes very hard to be racist, violent, prejudice, homophobic, anti-Semitic, misogynist, or oppressive when you live with an abundance of empathy. That's the simple solution to healing and fixing the world. One magic pill. That's all it would take.

You get to choose...

The red pill?
The blue pill?

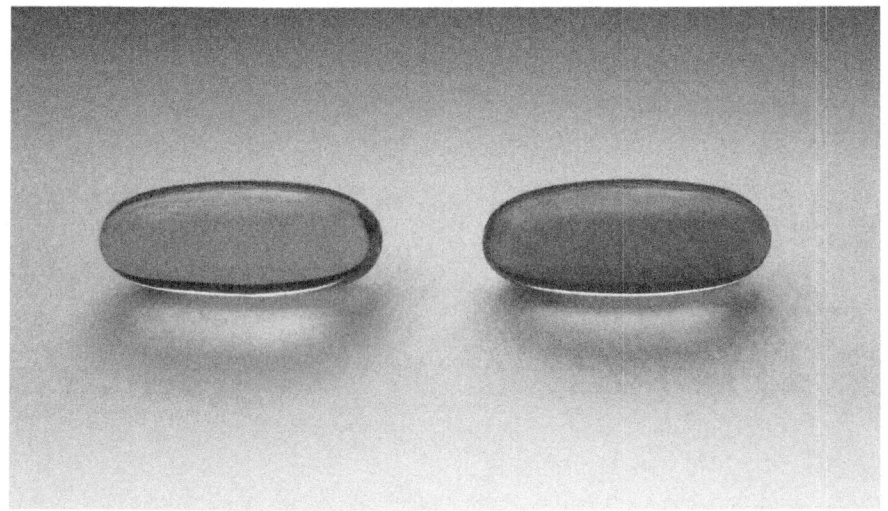

OR

the PINK Pill.

Because pink is the color of...

———————

Take a moment to evaluate the mindset and emotional state of those people in your close circle.

When was the last time you genuinely asked them how they were doing? And I don't mean on a casual level. I mean, having an intimate moment with them fueled by caring, vulnerability, and an overload of empathy.

I challenge you to choose one or two people this week and share more empathy.

Be more curious as to who they are and how they are doing deep down. The key to succeeding in this endeavor is to establish a safe and trusting connection. This may take time to build.
Copy, paste, repeat.

Chapter 14

The Long Road Back to Health (part 1)

The next three chapters are for both the person wanting to be more supportive to a friend during their emotional needs, and for the person who is in need of recovering from mental and emotional health situations.

There were a few angels along my road to recovery. They demonstrated great understanding void of judgment. I respect and honor their privacy and will, therefore, not mention them by name. One person's help was a thunderbolt of hope and relief that inspired me one day to pay it forward. This book is a part of my mission to save a life and pay it forward.

Thank you, kind angel, for the help and inspiration.

The process to survive and find myself again was long and painful. The journey was riddled with endless ups and downs. I dug deep. Deeper than at any other time in my life, determined. It pained me to admit that my childhood psychologists and statistics had predicted that I'd be dead or in jail due to crime, drugs or suicide. Those are the heavy burdens of an extremely abusive childhood.

If you have experienced intense emotional or psychological abuse, either in childhood or from a narcissist in childhood or adulthood, you are carrying some heavy trauma. That trauma is exhausting. It floods your body with high levels of cortisol (stress hormone), keeping you in perpetual high alert, or relentless fight of flight mode.

A part of your personal road to recovery will be to invest in highly focused, and intentional, emotional, spiritual and physical rest. As your body minimizes its cortisol levels, it will need to adapt in the same way one adapts after a long run or non-stop work. That's when the fatigue really hits you. Be good to yourself and don't ignore the need for extensive rest and recovery.

A part of the recovery is creating a new and healthy environment to soothe your soul. Your energy has been attracting a certain type of person. You might need to recreate an entire new circle of friends. The loss of so-called friendships will be painful. This is something you will have to take accountability for. Those selfish, advantage takers may not have been your fault, but they were always your responsibility. Find new friends who bring you peace. Become acutely aware of your nervous system and how you feel around certain people and certain environments. This new mindset is crucial to your healing.

You're almost starting life over again. The deeper the cleanse or purge, the better the odds of thriving on the other side. Remember, there will be setbacks and bad days. Keep going.

I had to go again and again, painfully scraping my knees as I temporarily regressed. I had to go again and gain re-evaluating my life, my choices, my habits.
There were many days of self-pity and self-doubt. Allow those moments to happen, always having empathy for YOU. Be kind to YOU.

It is an arduous journey to fight and overcome. The more support you can find, the better. I still struggle in this area… the journey never-ends because each new step, requires a new you to take the next step. Acknowledge and celebrate each step, each new boundary you establish.

I got help to go again from my new friends. It will be crucial to create a new circle of friends who are supporting, understanding and non-judgmental. Saying goodbye to the old friends and finding the right new ones is painful and lonely unto itself. Stay calm and carry on. One minute, one hour, one day at a time, celebrating the tiny victories. Sometimes the only victory to celebrate was getting out of bad and showering. One friend, in particular. His name is Kibo.

Chapter 15

The Long Road Back to Health (part 2)

Kibo means hope in Japanese. I met him when he was only four years old. A spirited soul who understood abandonment. Our eyes met one afternoon in November. From behind his caged confinement, he looked at me deep in the eyes and barked while wagging his tail with such vigor.

We spent twenty minutes in the dog run at the Lied Animal Foundation in Las Vegas. He ignored me for fifteen of those minutes.

I had just recently given up on life, and now a desperate dog was rejecting me. OUCH. Dejected, I signaled the assistant that we were done. As she made her way toward us, the long, white and black, Akita-Shepherd mix, stood up on his hind legs and placed his paws on my shoulders.

"Hi, daddy," he said. "I'm ready to save you if you take me home with you."

Kibo's empathy was beyond measure. Dogs are angels. They simply sit and lay WITH you. In many ways, all pets are angels. Due to my allergy to cats, they come in a close second. Animals and pets are magical. They save lives. I know for sure that dogs do because I have had many. I thought I was saving them. They were here for me as much as I was there for them.

Here are some pictures I share with great pride.

SALESIAN (Collie-Shepherd Mix)

SPIRIT: (White Shepherd)

LONDON and LADY BIANCA - Old English Sheepdog

MOCHA – Australian Shepherd

KIBO – Akita Shepherd Mix at Lied Animal Shelter

PINK IS THE COLOR OF EMPATHY

Becoming a high-value person in a disconnected world

KHARI – White Husky

All dogs are magical angels. If you're a cat lover, cats too are angels. Any pet that gives you love, and companionship is an angel. I don't discriminate.

———

"Dogs do speak, but only to those who know how to listen."

Orhan Pamuk

Chapter 16

The Long Road Back to Health (part 3)

Pets were not the only element that brought me back from deaths grip. The hard inner work continued. I created a list of 21 things to keep life positive, which you can read in my book, REACHING HIGHER.

One of those 21 things were dogs. Here are two more key elements.

1. VULNERABILITY

The challenge with being vulnerable is that it's scary, and who do you trust? Expose too much to the wrong person and they could set you back months. It's crucial to be vulnerable with the right person/people at the right time. How do you know?

> 1, Don't rush into trusting anybody.
> 2. Observe their character... patterns of behavior and energy give it away.
> 3. Intuition. Don't trust your intuition. Obey it.
> 4. Put out safe vulnerability feelers and observe what they do with what you've shared. If they meet your needs and expectations. Take another small risk. Over time you will get a good feel if this person can be trusted. It takes time. Be patient and diligent.
> 5. Intuition.
> 6. Take note of who is in that persons circle of friends. Who we surround ourselves with says everything about our character.
> 7. Intuition.

And you still might get it wrong. Learn, grow. Walk away when needed and start all over again. This is indeed a massive hurdle as it is hard to trust a world that has let you down. It is almost impossible to navigate the path of recovery alone. It takes a village/tribe and deep meaningful connection.

2. CBD and/or MICRODOSING

I have never done recreational drugs or drank alcohol, so why now? I personally view CBD or medical marijuana as exactly what it says... medicinal. The intention is specifically to heal, not to space or zone out. Be clear in this for yourself. This was my reasoning.

Before using microdosing, which is basically taking minute amounts of hallucinogenic mushrooms, speak to somebody who has great experience. Modern medicine is slowly embracing this, though perhaps not "enough" research and testing has been done. Some will argue that the side effects are dangerous. So are the side effects of any medication, in particular prescription anti-depressants... a contentious talking point I address later.

———

Chapter 17
Burn Out

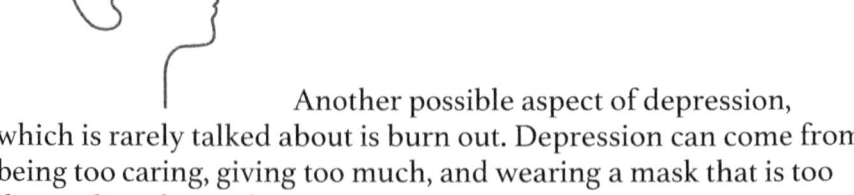

Another possible aspect of depression, which is rarely talked about is burn out. Depression can come from being too caring, giving too much, and wearing a mask that is too demanding, for too long.

Unfortunately, caring people are often taken advantage of, if not abused. This can deplete one's emotional fortitude, inspiring self-doubt if not self-loathing. Know thyself.

Do you give and care too much to the point it is detrimental to your wellbeing? This is common to empaths and people pleasers. Many empaths are people pleasers.

PINK IS THE COLOR OF EMPATHY
Becoming a high-value person in a disconnected world

What is an empath? It is a relatively modern term which we will talk about in depth further in the book.

What is people-pleasing?

———

Chapter 18

Do Nice Guys Finish Last?

 Hopefully, you're not a nice person or people-pleaser. Why?

Being kind and being nice are often used interchangeably to describe somebody's character. They are fundamentally very different, despite having overlapping traits. Just like cars have overlapping traits with planes (they transport people, they use fuel, they have engines, they need repairing, they can both crash), they are entirely different. Let's break it down.

What I'm about to share is more philosophical than scientifically factual. It is, however, a reality, or truth, in the sense that perception is reality.

PINK IS THE COLOR OF EMPATHY

Becoming a high-value person in a disconnected world

Allow me to ignore political correctness simply for the sake of making a point, and let's be boldly honest, "nice guys finish last!" Who even came up with that phrase? It's a common aphorism attributed to Brooklyn Dodgers manager, Leo Durocher. He used it to describe New Orleans baseball great, Mel Ott of the Giants, because since they sat bottom of the league that season in 1946. Leo Durocher "complimented" Mel Ott, saying, "Do you know a nicer guy than Mel Ott. Or any of the other Giants? And where are they? The nice guys over there are in last place!"

The phrase stuck!

It suggested lack of passion, desire, or grit to win; therefore, weak, submissive, easily pushed aside, not valued, or respected. Are nice guys undervalued, etc.? Whether or not they are factually undermined is irrelevant. They are perceived as weak. This applies to all genders and non-genders (to now be PC).

Let's go deeper.

There is another psychological level to bring to the table. Being nice suggests you are seeking approval or attempting to establish rapport. To seek approval, nice people will bend over backwards to accommodate the needs of others. They want to please them so that they are liked. This is manipulation. The nice person is being nice with one sole purpose. To seduce somebody into liking them or "acting" to gain favor. They are out to get or take something from you through a form of deceit. They NEED approval. If they need approval, they will compromise their values to gain that approval... to build rapport. This suggests a lack of integrity and authenticity.

Women have historically and stereotypically been characterized as putting and keeping nice men in the friend zone. Hence the perception that nice guys "don't get the girl." The PC version: a nice person won't get their romantic interest, because who wants to date the person at the bottom of the league.

Another area in which to establish a clear distinction between behaviors that are nice, as in manipulative or weak are: respect, empathy, sympathy, forgiveness, caring, etc. These are indeed nice, but they are not designed to seek approval. They are given by people who have decent amounts of confidence and emotional intelligence. They are an honor system rather than a stealth manipulation tactic based on insecurity and low self-esteem. Btw, some nice people have high self-esteem and don't necessarily seek approval. I would put those people, however, under the category of kind people.

Before you attack me for being insensitive and not a "nice guy," I have clearly stated the non-pc interpretation based on a phrase from the 1940s, "Nice guys finish last." It stuck and influenced our perceptions and decisions today.

If you are viewed as, or view yourself as a nice person who tends to please people and wish to change that, here's some help.
The two most frustrating side-effects of being a people-pleaser is that you exhaust yourself being so focused on the well-being of others. Resentment builds up over time. You can potentially become angry at them for "abusing you," OR, angry at yourself. Here's a harsh truth. You should be angry at yourself more than them. Why? Because you trained them and enabled them to treat you the way they do. Ouch!

Being a people-pleaser will slowly eat away at your soul and keep your self-esteem at a low level, inviting more people to abuse or take advantage of your over-zealous generosity. You have probably already reached this level if you're reading this. It's time to change for you own well-being.

It's going to take courage and time to overturn something that you've probably been doing your entire adulthood, if not starting in childhood. The good news is, you've got this. One step at a time. Let's begin this journey of transformation by identifying the top 10 traits of people-pleasers. This is a simplified bullet pointed list

PINK IS THE COLOR OF EMPATHY

Becoming a high-value person in a disconnected world

from a Psychology Today article by, Amy Morin, licensed clinical social-worker and psychotherapist.

1. You pretend to agree with everyone.
2. You feel responsible for how other people feel.
3. You apologize often.
4. You feel burdened by the things you have to do.
5. You can't say no.
6. You feel uncomfortable if someone is angry at you.
7. You act like the people around you.
8. You need praise to feel good.
9. You go to great lengths to avoid conflict.
10. You don't admit when your feelings are hurt.

You may or may not possess all these ten character traits. If you have multiple of these, then the odds are you are indeed a people-pleaser. If you are ready to transform into a more confident and decisive person, what comes next is for you. If you aren't ready, no worries, I am not here to please you. I am here to inspire and empower you to reach higher, grow wings and fly without a net.

How to stop being so nice (a people-pleaser)

How do I know all of this? Because I've travelled the journey, combined with extensive research. Coaching others to transform into more confident and decisive versions of themselves has also taught me much. I'm happy and honored to share.

1. **Set boundaries.**

   Be aware
   Of what is
   Unacceptable and
   Normalize saying no
   Do what is best for you
   And know that it's not your
   Responsibility to sacrifice
   Yourself for others

People pleasers tend to not set boundaries, let alone honor them. By not setting boundaries you are fully responsible for training people how to treat you. Learn and establish a goal to set boundaries at the onset of every single new relationship moving forward, starting today! Train yourself to say "no" to simple and seemingly meaningless things just for the hell of it. Get used to saying no! Train them to learn you are willing to say no. Focus on this as if your life depended on it, because it kind of does. Your wellbeing is on the line.

For the relationships that already know you to have non-existent boundaries, and who are already trained to know they can take advantage of you, establishing boundaries will cause great conflict. Be ready to experience conflict, even the death of those relationships. It's all necessary, so don't stop honoring your mission. It's going to suck. Keep at it.

2. **Stop looking for external validation.** This will take time and a lot of inner work to find the true source of self within you. Now, keep in mind, humans are social beings and our status and self-worth are influenced by how we are perceived and treated. However, deep down inside, you need to have a strong sense of self and self-worth. Take time to identify your strengths and stay focused on those things about you. Slowly minimize your need to rely on compliments to feel good about yourself. It's a process. If you start the work today and are consistent, you'll be surprised how quickly you can change.

3. **Be aware that you are trying to people-please.** All beginnings start with awareness that something is not the way you'd like it to be, and that change is required. Being honest with yourself and accepting that, yes, you are the "loser type, people-pleaser" will hurt and be upsetting. And ironically, that realization will weaken your already fragile self-esteem. Take the punch, a standing count. Get back up and begin the fight... today!

You once were a people-pleaser. That was yesterday. Today and tomorrow are different.

4. **Visualize yourself standing up for yourself.** Practice, practice, practice. It will take a while to get good at not people pleasing. Incremental steps and small weekly goals. Ask yourself, who do you people-please the most and begin changing those interactions with conviction and finesse.

   Those people will now be upset at your new boundaries. They may get (probably will get) angry and disappointed with you, claiming you've changed. Hell yeah, you've changed! The new you may even cost you relationships because they will no longer benefit from your exaggerated benevolence. Who wants to give up that kind of perk? Very few. *Dé-jà vu*??? Yes, I am intentionally repeating this. They could even try to manipulate you and accuse you of being mean, cold, and difficult.

   Don't become emotional! Logic and a cool head are required to navigate this selfish mirroring and blame shifting on their part. They know full well they took advantage of you. Be steadfast in your transformation. Keep going. New and better relationships are around the corner. Time to get a new tribe.

5. **You're not responsible for the feelings or problems of others.** You are not everybody's parent or babysitter. They are adults fully capable of making independent decisions and taking action to fix their problems and challenges. That shit is not your shit to fix!

6. **Honor yourself. Be KIND to yourself and live authentically.** Some will call this self-love. I prefer self-care and/or self-respect. As you honor yourself and establish new and solid boundaries, it may feel as if you are being mean. A hard "no" may sound insensitive and lacking empathy. Asking to have your needs and expectations met will feel aggressive to you. Keep going.

Allow the pendulum to potentially swing to the other extreme. In time, you will find the happy medium. But now, for once, it must be all about you. You've got this.

Having said all of this, please remember that in your mission to toughen up and stop being a people-pleaser, it's still okay, if not recommended, to **always be kind.**

———

If you don't implement consequences to people who violate your boundaries, you have in fact not set boundaries. You have set yourself up for manipulation if not abuse.

Chapter 19
The Gift of Kindness

Being kind can make you look like a "nice guy." So, what's the real difference? The intention and origin of an action and the presence of lack of healthy boundaries is the difference. Nice people lack boundaries. Kind people choose and select their boundaries wisely and enforce them while still being honorable. They choose their battles wisely, too. The toughest, most stoic, cold-hearted people are not nice as a rule, but they will be kind to those they love and respect. And the greatest of leaders will be kind if they want to empower others.

I hope you want to be a kind person.

When you are being kind, it shows a high level of Emotional Intelligence (EQ). You are choosing to be respectful and honor somebody else through your confidence, humility, and vulnerability (traits that are becoming highly valued in leaders and required in people we trust).

If you are a confident, successful, influential, and a powerful person, and can't be kind (to the waiter or those "below you"), then you're an asshole, or narcissist/sociopath.

Being kind is something you do for the greater good of humanity, whether you stand to gain or not.

Being nice is a need for validation. It's taking.

Being kind is a gift you bestow on others. It's giving on YOUR terms.

Always be kind.

Chapter 20
The Empath and Narcissist

In stark contrast to the kind or nice person, we have the narcissist. Common accepted belief by psychologists and clinical therapists is that what makes somebody a narcissist is the lack of empathy. Well, are you ready for controversy?

Remember I mentioned how FBI agents use "Tactical Empathy" during interrogations. This means they need to get into that prisoner's head in order to break them down or manipulate them into submission. And that's exactly what narcissists do. They get into your head. They play insidious mind games: gaslighting, triangulation, projecting, badgering, love bombing, deception, compulsive lying, breadcrumbing and ghosting.

If you are dealing with or have dealt with a narcissist and want to learn and understand more, I highly recommend researching online, or books, as to the sneaky manipulative complexities of their behavior and the consequences thereof. They can be devastating.

The only way a narcissist, let alone anybody, can get into somebody's head is to have empathy, even if it's only tactical empathy. They need to have an acute awareness and understanding of what their prey is thinking, feeling, and experiencing. Even if they don't emotionally feel the pain, they fully grasp the consequences of pain, tears, heartbreak and an ongoing mind-f$&#. They need to put themselves in the other person's shoes in order to have control. As ugly as that is, it is nonetheless, empathy.

What the narcissist lacks isn't empathy. They lack, compassion, guilt, shame, remorse, respect and kindness, although they know how to enact those behaviors or emotions to seduce their prey.

I love the breakdown in their differences by Dr. Rohit Barman. He says, "Both Empaths and Narcissists suffer from early developmental trauma. The difference is that Narcissists are essentially weak, and succumb to selfishness and hate, whilst Empaths rise above their torturous past, and continue to be there for humanity."

It has also been said and claimed that a narcissist cannot change. They are incurable. So don't be a nice guy or gal with them. Don't be patient, don't have compassion, don't forgive, or feel bad, and definitely don't have empathy for the narcissist. Run and don't look back. Go "no contact." In particular, if you are an empath.

What exactly is an empath, and what is the origin of the term?

That depends on which labels and theories you follow and believe in.

The term empath is relatively recent. Some claim its origins lie in science-fiction literature. Scottish author J.T. McIntosh's first sited the term in his 1956 story titled, "The Empath." It's a story about paranormally empathetic beings, called empaths. The government exploits their gifts of understanding others on a deep level. The objective is to control oppressed workers through these gifts of understanding and feeling.

Dictionary.com describes empath as: *(chiefly in science fiction) a person with the paranormal ability to apprehend the mental or emotional state of another individual.*

Depending on who and what you read, you will find different origins. Here are a few:

Empath stems from the word empathy but has a slightly different connotation.

Modern discussions debunk the concept of the empath. It is not an ability for the gifted, paranormal or superhuman. They suggest it is nothing more than hyper vigilance.

The hyper vigilance theory says that a child growing up in a traumatizing environment, with an abusive or narcissist parent, learns to pay attention to the subtle cues in mood and energy. Albert Mehrabian has a break down of communication percentages (see later). Well, the hyper vigilant are experts in identifying and interpreting the subtle shifts in verbal and non-verbal communication. It can sometimes be the nuance of the most minute change in the way the hairs on their dad's forearm stand. This could suggest a shift in blood pressure or internal body temperature, which means the onset of a bad mood, followed by a temper.

This is a skill that the average person would never even conceive let alone Identify... unless you're a trained Man in Black or FBI agent. Or your name is Bond, James Bond.

PINK IS THE COLOR OF EMPATHY
Becoming a high-value person in a disconnected world

Over time, this survival mechanism becomes subconscious and second nature. The acute observation happens within milliseconds. It then appears that they have this super ability to feel the pain, sense the energy and mindset of others. Is this true?

Regardless of calling them empaths, hyper vigilant or highly sensitive people (HSP), the result or outcome is the same. They can read or detect people's energy and moods. The problem with the hyper vigilance theory is it lacks explanation of sensing people who aren't present or visible.

Compare this to that innate sense that twins have when the other is experiencing something traumatic. Or twins separated at birth who both like specific clothes and food tastes. There is an energetic connection that science can't quite explain, given this is a genetic bond, but inexplicable, nonetheless. It's easy to deny something because we can't scientifically measure or repeat it in a test tube. Well, I think empaths can't yet be explained or proven. So, they find a term that explains the inexplicable.

I prefer to not focus on the label because it undermines the ability to read and understand (or feel) people.

The empath navigates life with a blessing or curse dependent on perception and the ability to understand and leverage what they possess.

If it's true that empaths can feel and absorb the energy of others, it can be a heavy burden to carry because they are bombarded from everywhere with energy that is not theirs. Not only is that confusing, it's also overwhelming. It can lead to mental and social disorders such as depression and/or anxiety. Maybe it's like being able to see dead people and people think you're insane.

If the empath learns to understand what they are feeling and can protect themselves and feel but not absorb external energy and emotions, then it becomes a gift. The key to optimizing their ability is to physically, spiritually, and emotionally build a force-field or protective bubble that doesn't allow negative energy to penetrate.

Top 12 Traits of an Empath (not in order of importance or value)

1. Highly intuitive (sometimes psychic).
2. Deep love and connection to animals and nature.
3. Attract energy vampires, narcissists.
4. Often introverted.
5. Very sensitive to all external factors and emotions (HSP).
6. Intimacy can be scary, even overwhelming.
7. Need plenty of solitude and introspection time.
8. Crowds and loud noises can be hard to manage.
9. Acute awareness of micro-communication and subtle shifts in energy, intention, mood etc.
10. Are a healing light source of goodness, patience and kindness. Often, too much compassion for their own wellbeing.
11. Prone to anxiety and depression resulting in isolation.
12. Wounded souls feel safe with you and share abundantly.

A repeated ingredient empaths need in order to function on a healthy and beneficial level is to set **boundaries**. The need for **boundaries** is also crucial for the extra kind or nice people (the people-pleasers).

Empaths tend to care too much. They take on the problems of others through listening with an excess of concern. They compromise if not sacrifice their own well-being to help and please others. This is exhausting and depleting.

With such a gift of understanding and feeling the pain of others, doesn't mean that they can or do communicate that caring. Some empaths feel but remain silent or distant. Empathy has very little value if it is not communicated and understood by the recipient.

If you are an incredibly sensitive person, you may be an empath, or hyper vigilant. Regardless of which label you subscribe to, take time to research this in great depth and learn to make it your friend. Your ability can provide incredible levels of healing to a highly disconnected and overall depressed world. Your abilities make you a high-value person, but again, only if you learn to optimize the ability.

If you become depleted, you serve little purpose to yourself, let alone others. Become an empowered empath!

Chapter 21

The Nine Pillars of Empathy

So, what does empathy look, sound, feel and taste like?

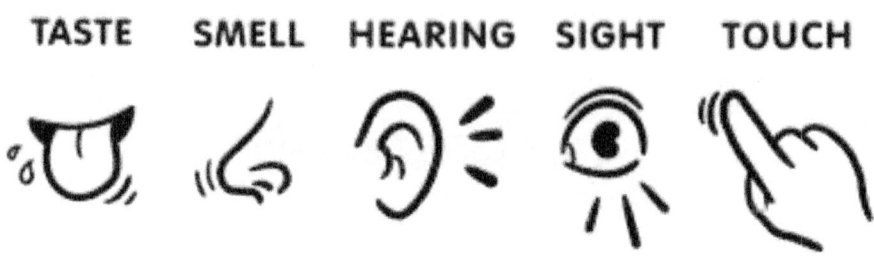

Empathy consists of multiple key ingredients that unto themselves are not empathy.

The following behaviors are not necessarily synonyms of empathy, but rather traits that we will more likely demonstrate or experience due to the sharing of empathy.

1. Respect

The word respect derives from the Latin *respects*. It means: "regard, looking at," literally "act of looking back (or often) at one," as in, "I see you."

To truly see somebody, we must take the time and be curious enough to understand them. How do you understand somebody? By putting yourself in their shoes and seeing things from their perspective.

Respect may be the ultimate form of empathy and one of the most honorable gifts you can share with somebody. Time and attention are the only rivals to respect. We all love feeling respected. We all love it when people see us, hear us... get us. It validates our existence. In fact, the Zulu tribe of South Africa has a term that sums this up. It's called, *Sawubona*. It literally means, "I see you." According to their beliefs we don't exist until we are seen. Letting somebody know you see them brings them into existence validating everything about them. The gift of *Sawubona* is a beautiful and powerful gift. It gives us a sense of belonging. It honors us with significance, from which we can build meaning, purpose and fulfillment.

I see YOU.

Sawubona.

2. Compassion

As a result of having empathy for somebody we will be inclined to have compassion. We might be gentler in how we treat them or judge them. The greatest of Roman emperors were admired and revered whenever they showed compassion. It's a delicate dance between perceiving compassion as a strength or weakness.
The same dance applies to empathy, unfortunately.

3. Generosity

We often associate generosity with donating money or sharing our resources with abundance. Empathy has no monetary value, yet it is priceless. Any form of giving from the heart is a blessing to those who receive.

You may have heard of stories of people paying for the order of a random stranger or giving a homeless person food or money. These are all beautiful and admirable gestures that change lives.

Sometimes our actions and words are gifts to somebody in need. We may never know the positive impact of what we do and say.

Through social media I have been able to reconnect with some very influential role models during my youth and teens. Their generosity and empathy saved my life.

The first was a black woman, a staff member at the home (institution). She instilled in me a pride of being black. I was confused and lost as a biracial kid living in a predominantly white neighborhood and attending effectively all white schools. The way she carried herself reminded me of how I remembered my mother once used to be. Dignified, elegant and strong, all the while being kind and respectful.

The second, my English teacher in elementary school. She took me to the theatre and the opera. She cared for me and made me feel valued and special midst the sea of rejection that kids face living in a group home. I can thank her for having planted the seed that led to an amazing five-year stint with Cirque du Soleil.

The third, a community worker who wasn't paid to overlook us. He spent time with me and other kids in the home on his own dime. He understood us. He cared. He made a difference.

The fourth, the owner of a nightclub in Blankenberge. It's a small coastal town in Belgium. He hired me when nobody else would. Why would nobody hire me? I'm going to argue it was a racial thing. I was one of three non-whites who lived in this town of about fifteen thousand inhabitants. Racism hurts. That job was a game-changer for me. It helped me escape the grasp of my narcissist and sexually abusive father.

The fifth, was a friend who helped my turn a dream into reality. With her support, I ran away from the tiny town in Belgium to pursue my dream. Welcome to America. Welcome to New York.

There have been many more helpers along my journey. I think we all have significant helpers in our lives--givers. I'm sure you do, if you look back.

Perhaps the most significant helper was my elementary school P.E. teacher. He and his wife took me under their wing. I spent many weekends with them. My best Christmas memories were when we visited their parents in the north of England. They felt like family.

The emotional generosity of all the above, have helped shape who I am and shaped my dreams. I am forever grateful. Generosity is a beautiful thing.

Did you ever watch the movie, Pay it Forward? In many ways, my career choices and this book are my way of paying it forward, in the way that I know how.

4. Caring

Empathy is now being taught in some schools. This is great news. There is hope for us all. For some, empathy is an innate character trait, for others it's learned behavior. Here's how it impacts you in the workplace as an employee, leader, or customer. Empathy is a very clear and effective way to let somebody know you care. If you care, you will highly likely do what's right for that person. As a result of caring, you will have their back. This makes you trust-worthy... a high-value person.

Anthony Gucciardi, a natural health and human empowerment writer, speaker, and entrepreneur says, "Empathy is the highest form of intelligence." In an age when Emotional Intelligence (EQ) is becoming more relevant than ever (a trend), it is a gift that needs to be promoted and elevated by leadership as a requirement.

Looking like you care even if you don't.

If you genuinely care, everything falls naturally into place. If you don't care, it's a challenge. Here are some tips to help you appear as if you care. Hopefully if you do this overtime, you will begin to care.

i. Kindness & Friendliness

The good news is that even people who don't care, know how to be kind, polite, and friendly. These are traits of people who do care. They are behaviors that can be taught or "faked". If practiced often, they become your new lifestyle.

Implement the "21/90 Rule" for best transformation results.

The 21/90 Rule states that it takes twenty-one days to develop a new habit: good or bad. And we all know that habits are easily broken. Don't believe me; think of your New Year's Resolution. They rarely last two weeks. In fact, I saw a meme on this topic. "I'm going to open a gym called Resolutions. It will turn into a bar two weeks after opening." Business will probably be great.

If you honor a new behavior (habit) for ninety days, it becomes a lifestyle. Lifestyles stick because it means we've become that new behavior. It's more about being than doing.

ii. Smiling

A smile is so easy to share... even if you don't care. It's a powerful tool. A smile is the most recognized non-verbal expression of goodness. A smile says that you are inviting a connection. It suggests you will be helpful and caring. I've seen the most indifferent people smile and look like they actually care. Danish musician, conductor and comedian, Victor Borge said, "A smile is the shortest distance between two people." Smiles are contagious if not infectious. Share many, often.

iii. Curiosity

There are two types of curiosity. There is the being nosey and getting all up in people's business, ignoring boundaries and privacy. That type is not healthy and not what I am promoting.

Then there is the type of curiosity which is based on benevolence and desire to better understand somebody. Your intentions are pure. It comes from a place of love and trust, a desire to bring value to a person. By being curious about somebody, you find commonality; you build rapport.

As the relationship deepens and you know more about their personality, you start to view them differently because you have a deeper understanding of their journey, motives, and quarks.

Your curiosity will also help you understand if you're a good fit. If you're not a good fit, no foul, no harm. Move on respectfully with minimal judgment, maintaining only healthy boundaries.

5. Inspiration
Sometimes, empathy is your behavior as an example for somebody to look up to. It's not the same as motivation. Motivation doesn't work when trying to be empathetic. Motivation makes it about your mindset and not theirs. Motivation can be toxic positivity to the person in need of understanding.

"My _____ just cheated on me."
"Ah don't worry, there are plenty more fish in the sea and they weren't worthy of you." This is toxic positivity posing as empathy. It can often have the opposite effect as you expected. They might not show it, but subconsciously, they may feel resentment. You've undermined their pain because you're not hurting and your all optimistic and happy.

The goal, here is to spark a desire in them to change perspective, or incite desire to learn, grow and change. If they've witnessed you handle disappointment with grace and resilience, they may try to emulate you. That's inspiration and not motivation. Vulnerability is a great means to inspire somebody. Furthermore, inspiration does not put pressure on anybody because it's all about their own choice and in their own time. When they are ready to take action they will. Your job is to plant a seed for them, not be the flower.

6. Relatability
If we can see ourselves in the situation, it will feel like empathy, though it may not be. Be careful with this one. Don't communicate your relatability by sharing your similar story and then hogging the conversation... which many do. Even if done harmlessly and

with good intentions, it's not empathy. You will have then made it about YOU. Empathy is never about you. It's always about them during that time of need.

7. Sympathy

Empathy is often confused with sympathy. There is commonality between the two, yet the difference in meaning is beyond a nuance or a synonym. The difference is, in fact, substantial. Empathy means you feel their suffering. Sympathy means you understand their pain without actually feeling it. Sympathy means I feel bad FOR you. Empathy means I feel bad WITH you.

Furthermore, sympathy can turn into pity, and pity can be toxic. Pity doesn't inspire or elevate. It degrades somebody. People rarely want pity. They want to be seen, heard and understood. Pity or sympathy left unchecked can become enabling. It promotes a victim mentality, which doesn't help long term. And who wants that kind of energy in their life?

8. Listening

Listening is a fine skill if not an art form. There are five types of listening. Each one brings a different form of value. And we all do these at different times for different reasons with different people. Understanding these five different types of listening will give you an advantage, inspiring positive outcomes.

i. Ignoring

We all know what ignoring looks, sounds, and feels like. It sucks when we are being ignored. It makes us feel unworthy, insignificant, invisible, and unloved.

Did you know that when the person you love, or whose attention means the world to you, ignored you the pain can manifest in physical form via tension in the chest and literal heartache? The only people that deserve to be ignored are those who repeatedly disrespect you, use you, or manipulate you. If that person is a narcissist, then ignore them to the point of what is called, NO CONTACT.

The more recent term for ignoring somebody is "GHOSTING." If they are ignoring you, you are being "GHOSTED." It hurts. Try to let it go and move on as quickly as possible to protect your mental and emotional wellness.

If you are superficially ghosting somebody, have empathy and understand how painful it could be to them. Reevaluate if ghosting them is necessary. Good, open communication could resolve the issue.

ii. Pretend Listening

We have all pretended to listen at some point. Probably more than we care to admit. This is a soft form of ignoring. The other person is oblivious to the fact they are being ignored.

We pretend to listen for endless reasons like being preoccupied with other thoughts or being polite when we really don't care or have the time to listen.

iii. Selective Listening

This is the ugly twin of pretend listening. If you have kids, you will know exactly what this form of listening is. You will listen selectively yourself. Your kids will listen selectively. It's just one of those things we do in life.

iv. Active or Attentive Listening

This type of listening is the one we are usually taught to do. It's the standard and believed to be highly impactful. And in many ways, it is.

Active listening means we are paying attention and hearing the other person. We are perhaps doing all the right things to communicate our attention: we lean in, we nod in acknowledgment, we might even mirror them (mimicking their body language or energy).

We may even be listening with so much attention that we could repeat their words verbatim. This would be highly impressive. BUT!

If you heard every word they said, but you still don't care, then what?

Listening attentively will have served very little purpose. You may as well have pretended to listen. If you listen to somebody and don't care for what they had to say, you wasted both your time and their time because you can now bring little value in terms of the next step.

v. Empathetic Listening

Listening without empathy has little meaning, even if you heard everything I said. Unless you care and feel what I just shared, it was basically a monologue.

Listening fueled by empathy means you understand me. We are on the same page. We have connected on a deep level. Only then does our listening really bring deep value. Listening with empathy makes you a high value person.

On a professional level in the workplace, it's the ultimate first step in leadership and customer service. We must CARE in order to bring value.

Who in your life needs, deserves your empathetic ear void of judgment or motivation? Who needs you to be Brother Christian to Matthew McConaughey? Give it a try with somebody in your life with whom you desire a more significant connection. Document the changes in your relationship. I hope they reciprocate. If not, give them this book.

9. Understanding

As was mentioned earlier in the sympathy section, understanding is complicated, yet it is the doorway to empathy.

The other important aspect of understanding is that it doesn't mean we agree or condone.

"I get it. I still think you're an %&@."

It's easy to understand something that we've experienced. It's a matter of seeing and identifying the reflection in the mirror. Understanding that which is different is the real test. That means eliminating: the ego, conscious and subconscious biases, preconceived notions, stubborn and one-sided belief systems, social-economic status, religious or political persuasions, all of which evoke "cognitive dissonance."

In short, cognitive dissonance is the inability to let go of something. Scientifically it means that neural pathways are fixed/stuck. The brain is unable to create new ones. This can make us narrow-minded or stubborn--or blind--not "woke" or forward thinking. It's all relative.

How narrow-minded of me to think you narrow minded! Oh, the irony, if not hypocrisy.

Overcoming these hurdles is no easy task to achieve. Negating cognitive dissonance is in fact one of the hardest things for human beings to do. We grasp onto that which we know and believe in. Those beliefs have defined our lives: our choices, our friends, our careers, and so forth. They can negate the ability to empathize despite good intentions.

Without any levels of empathy, it becomes almost impossible to understand somebody who has a different perspective, philosophy, life experience, or different core values than you.

The movie *Wonder,* staring Owen Wilson and Julia Roberts, explores the concepts of how we behave and make decisions. The film takes you on the journey of a young boy whose face is heavily deformed. As a result of his deformity, he wears an astronaut's helmet to hide from kids at school, and even his own family.

Initially, you see life from his perspective. He encounters a few stereo types: the arrogant kid who seems to have it all, and who looks down on him, and the spoiled pretty girl who gets the boy and the lead in the school play over his sister. The director reveals the personal struggles of each kid.

The pretty girl has an identity issue because her mother is an alcoholic and her father doesn't have time for her. So, she becomes miss congeniality to compensate.

The arrogant spoiled boy has narcissist parents who have given him a bad example of entitlement due to their wealth. And the boy with the deformity has a sister that has always lived in his shadow. Mom and dad were always making it about him. She was invisible.

Seeing each of their struggles changes your opinion of them. That's the value of being curious about people. Getting to know their story changes who you thought they were. Empathy will help you see them differently. Seeing them differently means you will treat them differently. What a beautiful ripple effect.

Chapter 22
Gifting

For the most part, we all crave the same things. We all want to receive such things as: love, respect, generosity, kindness, understanding, belonging, compassion, and forgiveness. Unfortunately, many are unable or unwilling to give. Empathy is about giving. It is generous. It is kind. It is respectful. It is the most valuable of gifts.

There is a conundrum with gifting and making **empathy** all about them.

PINK IS THE COLOR OF EMPATHY

Becoming a high-value person in a disconnected world

If you subscribe to Russian philosopher Ayn Rand, the act of giving is selfish. Her platform of objectivism claims that everything we do is ultimately for personal gain. Those who give do so because it makes them feel good. Which means they are rewarded for their giving, and it's this feel-good factor that is a selfish motivation, according to Ayn Rand.

Whether objectivism is true or not, the gift of empathy brings great value to society. In a perfect world, we'd all be giving and feeling great about ourselves. Empathy is great and powerful in all aspects of life, at home and at work.

Empathy is not a weakness. It only becomes a liability if it compromises your values. It only becomes a liability if you are unable to establish healthy **boundaries.** Remember that such self-sacrificing givers are referred to as "people pleasers" or "nice people." They are taken-advantage of, if not abused. They must set healthy boundaries.

A healthy boundary is not words. It is action with consequences if and when you are not respected or honored. If there are no consequences to bad behavior, you have not established boundaries, you have simply set yourself up for more abuse. **Boundaries must have consequences.** You can forgive and not allow that person back into your life. This is sometimes the necessary boundary.

The great gift of human beings is that we have the power of empathy.

Meryl Streep

Having empathy is one thing. Gifting or communicating empathy is another.

How do you let people know you have empathy, feel their pain, care and are there for them?

This challenge is not as evident as you might think. Really analyze how you communicate your empathy. Is it clearly felt and understood?

Empathy isn't synonymous with agreement. It also doesn't mean you are obliged to be forgiving or nice.

Chapter 23
Just Say Something

Oh, btw, that dream I had regarding slashing my wrists, wasn't a nightmare. I had slit my wrists. For real! The sharp blade had pierced my skin multiple times.

I cut my left wrist first. I felt dizzy. My forehead became warm. I smiled at the thought that my earthly suffering was ending. It wasn't a nightmare. It was real. I had cut my wrist. The dizziness faded.

I moved the box cutter away from my left wrist to my right for a better and deeper cut.

Aargh.

Back to my right wrist for a third cut. And another switch.

Nobody would understand!

That thought validated my reason to leave this cold, selfish planet.

I became dizzy again, though much more intensely, and closed my eyes. My heart filled with relief. My forehead became hot. My mouth a desert terrain. I lost all strength in my body and laid my head back. Reality blurred and darkened into a muted tunnel. The suffering was ending. I neither saw my life flashing before me nor did a bright light in the distance beckon me.

I woke up approximately twenty minutes later in the bathtub, dazed, drenched in blood, confused, and disappointed. Then I panicked.

The vision of a few people I loved deeply flashed through my mind. I didn't want to die. I never wanted to die. I wanted to live. I just wanted the pain to end. Fighting it for a lifetime had exhausted me.

I want to live.

This was very much an in-body experience. Perhaps an out-of-my damned-bloody-mind experience, dare I say, to humorously minimize the gravity of my choice. Humor has always helped me handle stress and trauma. I laugh at my own psychosis, not with others'.

"Just say something," I've heard many say.

"Why didn't you just tell me?"
"We love you and would have been there for you."

Blah, blah, blah.

If only it were that simple to, to simply say something. You are trivializing the trauma, guilt, and shame of the suicidal. If people could handle the simple act of saying something, it would mean they hadn't yet reached the end of the line where they were unable to handle a single additional burden or pain point. Don't add responsibility and accountability to their dire situation. That is simply asking too much. Instead of placing the burden on the deeply wounded and broken, we should place that burden on society to be me more sensitive, aware and caring of those in need. That's almost like asking somebody who is illiterate to send an application to a school so they can learn to read and write.

Ever since that Saturday morning at around 10:30am on November 21st of 2015, I have struggled to process and embrace the great shame associated with it. I have continued living with internal disgrace at the lie of hiding what I did for too long. The consequences of my actions could be costly. It has chewed my heart and mind inside out, devouring my integrity.

It has taken me this long, seven years, perhaps too long, to go public and turn my darkest pain into the ultimate purpose of the human experience. To save and prolong another life that is clinging to their last embers of hope.

In writing this book and revealing my greatest shame, I am filled with almost paralyzing fear to "just say something."

I am ready for judgment!

PINK IS THE COLOR OF EMPATHY

Becoming a high-value person in a disconnected world

Next to creating a life, the finest thing a man can do is save one.

Abraham Lincoln

Chapter 24
Labels and Belief

For those who believe in God, it is perhaps a miracle that I am alive. I don't believe in God. I do believe that a divine entity or higher universal power, or even computer assimilation (or aliens), had decided that today was not a good day to die. We possibly believe in the same thing with a different label and with different constraints. Either way, that entity, regardless of its cosmic identity, gave me a second chance!

Despite my lack of religious conviction, I hope you will pray for me and others. I'm not sure that prayers and thoughts have ever really impacted the universe and changed the course of destiny, other than the fact that collective prayer is a form of focused energy by a group of people that may have an effect. I'll take a prayer or other forms of light energy over judgment and condemnation, as will most who have or who are considering suicide.

Can I get an amen?

Thank you.

Ultimately, empathy is a great place to start.

Remember, I never wanted to die. I just wanted the torment to end. I wish I could have just shared. I wish I had simply said something. But it's so hard to share. It felt impossible.

Some of you may be thinking (judging) and suggesting this act was a cry for help or attention. It was not. This moment had been on my mind for days. I had planned it and visualized it with every intention to succeed. That is how much my soul was suffering. It had been suffering for years and years... in silence. The decision to end it scared the crap out of me. I'm not sure I had ever experienced fear to this intensity. I had never planned my death before.

Was I mentally deranged? Was I mentally ill? I had never wanted to die. Controversy warning!

Mental wellness and emotional wellness overlap but are two very separate issues. We place them both under the same umbrella. Which means they are viewed and "treated" as the same. We prescribe medication, too quickly sometimes.

I, personally, have an issue with anti-depressants. I lack the mental capacity to comprehend how a medication that has suicide as a potential side-effect is allowed on the market. Surely, the pharmaceutical industry should be mandated to improve this product. The irony of my attempted suicide is that a week prior I had been prescribed an anti-depressant. Within days of taking them, I felt a drastic and extremely negative swing in my mood. The darkness intensified by the minute. I felt heaviness and desperation like I had never felt before. I didn't know who I was. Hyper-anxious one minute, numb the next, and then manic, and then the sudden histrionic emotional drop that prompted my actions, spurred by several days of almost zero sleep. I don't remember getting a whole night's sleep since I started taking the antidepressants.

Riddle me this again. How is a medication that has as a side-effect, suicidal thoughts, allowed on the market? Pharmaceutical industry, you can and should do better! FDA, you can and should do better.

Can I blame it entirely on my antidepressants? No. However... if a phone battery has a side-effect of potentially combusting, it is recalled. If a car has a side-effect or defect of breaks failing, they are recalled. If a plane has an engine issue leading to crashes, they are what? Yes, they are recalled. Yet a medication that has a side-effect of death is heavily prescribed and not recalled.

Perhaps, one day, a major lawsuit will be filed when enough people realize this. The thought has crossed my mind though logically, I understand the miniscule odds of winning against a financial behemoth with expansive political clout.

Prozac®, or fluoxetine, was approved December of 1987 by the FDA. in December of 1987. In January of 1988, it became available on the market. In 2018, the manufacturer of Prozac®, Teva Pharmaceuticals, recalled its own product, due to irregular testing results. Oh! So, there was a "recall." Apparently without fixing the suicidal thoughts as a side-affect part.

In the 1950s, iproniazid, was the first clinically introduced drug to the antidepressant family. It's a monoamine-oxidase inhibitor.

Monoamine-oxidase is associated with the removal of the neurotransmitters, norepinephrine, serotonin and dopamine from the brain--"happiness" hormones.

Let me be clear! Despite my criticism of anti-depressants and the pharmaceutical industry, I am fully aware that anti-depressants bring great value to many. They have probably saved many lives. If you are on meds, please continue taking them and seek counseling. I am only expressing an opinion that is not based on science.

And CBD or marijuana are/were illegal at the time? It makes no sense to me. Btw, I chose CBD for a while after my attempt. It helped. It saved my life. I am not addicted. It was not a gateway drug. It simply eliminated the suicidal thoughts. What irony, take a pill to eliminate a symptom, but the side-effect of said pill could inspire the very symptoms you are fighting. Such insanity and confusion is depressing.

I'd experienced depression before that gloomy day of November 21st, 2015. I'd been confused and broken before. I had experienced the loss of desire to live, but I had never had suicidal thoughts. I had never lost hope... until the meds kicked in. I didn't recognize myself. Ultimately, I am accountable and responsible on all levels. However, allow me to rationalize my choice.

It took a series of drastic and dramatic events to happen over the span of several years. I'm going to say it was seven jinxed years to throw in some theatrical dust and dramatic intrigue.

1. A divorce.
2. A change/end to my S-Corp. The company hit a financial hurdle as the economy changed.
3. The loss of two Old English Sheepdogs (Bianca and London) within weeks of each other. I'd had them for thirteen and fourteen years.

4. Financial strain: on the verge of losing my house.
5. Adopted a rescue dog (unplanned) that had medical issues. Lost him within six months of the other two.
6. A relationship with a narcissist woman. The relationship was plagued with the standard behaviors of a narcissist: love-bombing, gaslighting, triangulation, benching, ghosting, and one-upping. This experience unto itself may have been the metaphoric and almost literal nail in my coffin.
7. Anti-depressants, that pushed my mood over the edge.
8. A childhood that had predicted I'd die of suicide, if not drugs or crime.

The sad part for me is that I had defied the odds of childhood statistics with great resolve and resilience for so long. I guess they knew what they were talking about after all.

I still believe that it was an emotional deficit that pushed me over the edge. During my trials (see list), I felt like I had very few people I could trust enough to share with. I had a very small support system to provide emotional reinforcement.

Over the years, I have had many bouts of depression. Maybe, like the Hulk, who is always angry, I am perhaps always mildly depressed. The triggers have usually been a sense of disconnect and loneliness. Whenever I have felt love, security, and purpose, I have been filled with life and vigor. In perfect alignment with Maslo's Hierarchy of needs.

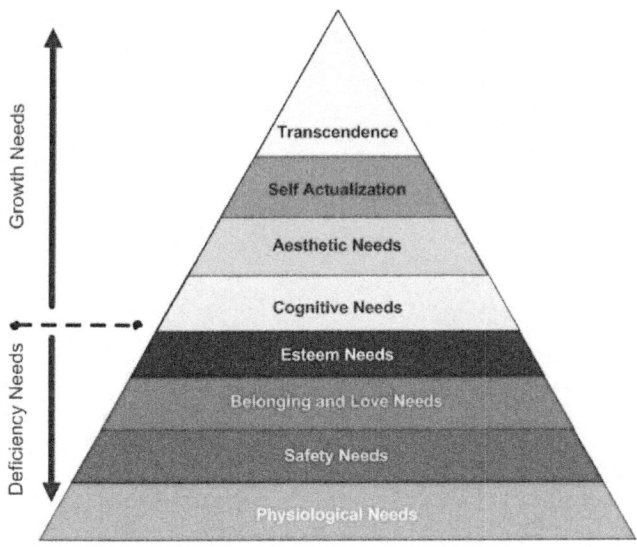

I blame it on an unresolved accumulation of emotional depravity. In due time, that does indeed become mental illness. Think of pirates and sailors who would lose their teeth and experience gum disease--scurvy, savvy.

They focused on the wrong issue and determined that apples were needed. The "root" cause (pun intended) was a lack of vitamin C. There is perhaps a major similarity between emotional and mental health. Not all mental health has the same root cause, yet "apples" were prescribed for both. Food for thought (pun intended, again).

To reiterate, my findings of the negative attributes of anti-depressants are purely based on personal experience and opinion. They are neither scientific nor clinical, due to the fact that, I am not a scientist or medical expert. Beyond my personal experience, I only have read, including internet research to back my claims. I don't recommend following my suggestions but rather seeking counsel from a qualified advisor. Having said that, there is never any harm in doing a little personal research and seeking explanation from a physician as to how or why they have come to any given conclusion or diagnosis. Doctors and medical experts have failed miserably before and will fail miserably again.

Chapter 25
It Takes a Village

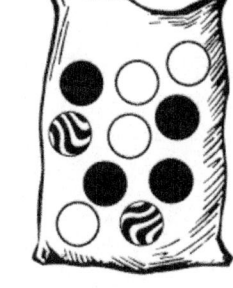

Doing my best to face my shadows and deny societal judgments, I lumbered back into my safe sanctuary of silence and isolation.

The odd friend that I trusted, displayed everything other than empathy. I had chosen the wrong people to be vulnerable with. They challenged my perception of reality... only adding to my emptiness, brokenness, and guilt. They questioned my character and choices. Some didn't believe the evils I shared about my narcissist girlfriend who was systematically destroying my soul. My own friends were gaslighting me.

Playing devil's advocate, they call that. I think it's called being an insensitive asshole or prick when a friend is sharing his pain. It's so easy to do. When unpeeling the empathy onion, it's evident that it's not only about listening. We must also believe their pain, situation and perception. Perception is reality.

The same friends kept highlighting the positive things I should focus on. They were being cheerleaders.

"There's plenty of fish in the sea, Vital." That's the last thing I wanted or needed to hear. I understood their intentions. But! The dark hole simply grew in depth and obscurity.

It's me. I'm a nut job who's lost his marbles. I am the problem. I am a freak.

Regarding my narcissist ex, beware! The term narcissist is loosely used for people who are selfish. Narcissists are indeed selfish, but what they suffer from is not a behavior problem, it is a serious and diagnosed mental health disorder. It is incurable. Narcissism is too often associated as a toxic male issue. The toxic female (narcissist) exists, too. She has lived under the radar, undetected way too long. Her iniquities are under documented. She has been known to drive men to insanity, financial ruin, and suicide.

Unless you have experienced the wrath of a person with Narcissist Personality Disorder (NPD) or Borderline Personality Disorder (BPD), you may have trouble fathoming the extent of their evilness. I am far from a psychiatrist or licensed therapist, though I think my previously mentioned ex may have suffered from a bit of both.

A few recent pop culture stories have begun to expose the covert and overt female narcissist's conniving and well-hidden darkness. Be informed so that you may avoid her, if not any gender (or non-gender) of narcissist, like the plague.

Just like with all previous historical cultural shifts, it takes a collective to inspire let alone enforce a change in thinking, perception, and behavior. The change can be initiated by a single person, but it needs a large enough of a group of people who have become aware to incite a tipping point. The key to this, despite the evil of a narcissist, is still to understand and not condemn. Again, think boundaries. You can understand, forgive but still keep them at a safe distance without the need or desire for revenge or condemnation.

It also takes more than one person to share empathy to a spirit in need to have an effective impact. In other words, the larger the support group or tribe is, the quicker the healing and recovery happens. It literally takes a village. It takes a caring, non-judgmental village that doesn't punish, condemn or seek retribution.

BABEMBA TRIBE

The Babemba tribe of South Africa has unique approach to bad behavior. When a person behaves poorly or unjustly, they are brought to the center of the village unrestrained. All work stops and every man, woman, and child in the village gathers. They create a large circle around the accused individual. Each person in the tribe speaks to the accused, one at a time. Each person bring up the good things the accused did in their lifetime: each situation, every experience that can be remembered with any detail and accuracy, is shared. All their positive traits, positive deeds, strengths, and kindnesses are recalled carefully and at great length. This tribal ritual can last for days.

To conclude tribal circle, they celebrate. That guilty person is symbolically and literally welcomed back into the tribe.

This is beautiful and utopian and may not function in our western society, however, there is much to learn from this mindset on how to handle hurt people. Because it is hurt people who act out, usually as a rebellion to their pain and suffering.

There is an African proverb that says, "The child who is not embraced by the village will burn it down to feel its warmth."

One of the most painful things a human can experience and have their psyche destroyed is the rejection from a community they depend on.

———

Chapter 26
Negativity Is So Negative

People run away from negativity. They avoid dark, dull objects that suck and absorb the light. And I am not free of this behavior. Through introspection I have become more aware of getting caught up in social pressures to be fun, cool, and happy.

Everywhere I turned were reminders of how nobody wanted to be around negativity. It simply magnified my pain and my sense of aloneness.

Social media has magnified that "toxic positivity," as I call it. We fake and pretend, pretend, and fake. Smile for a snapshot when we're crying inside. Some people are genuinely happy.

We post memes that make us look positive, happy, and successful. Memes that will inspire people to like us 'cause we've got our shit together. People are attracted to success and confidence. People LIKE shiny objects that elevate their self-worth, even if only by association.

PINK IS THE COLOR OF EMPATHY

Becoming a high-value person in a disconnected world

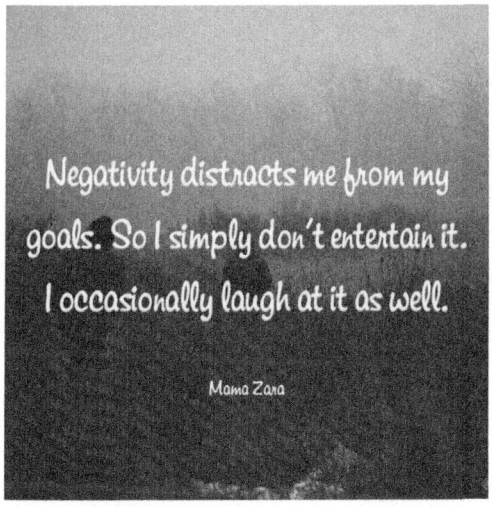

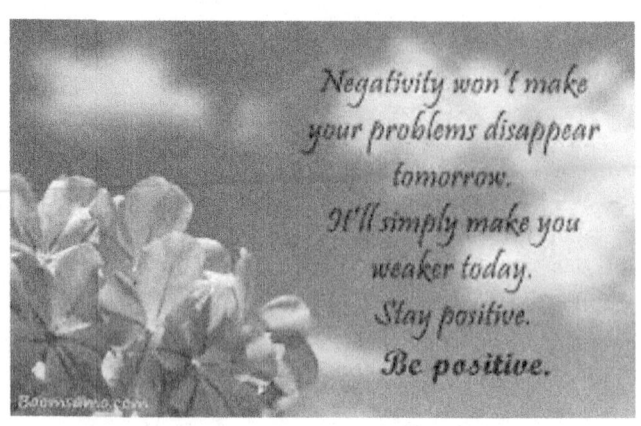

PINK IS THE COLOR OF EMPATHY

Becoming a high-value person in a disconnected world

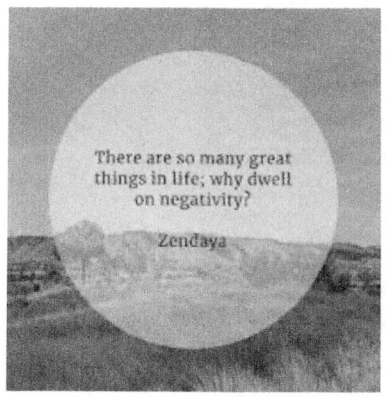
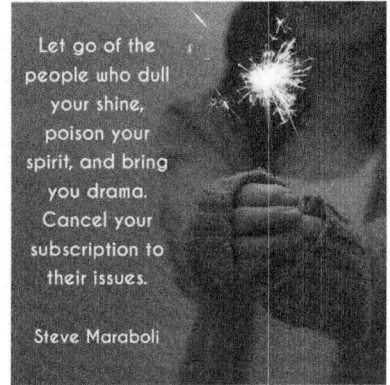

> I have no time for negativity, I have way too much to be grateful for. Remove the stress and realize you're blessed.

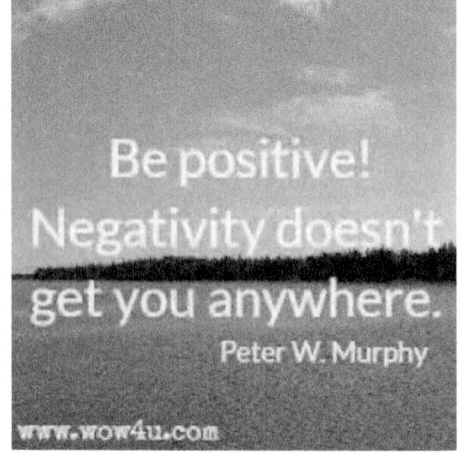

I am all for optimism, hope, and a positive mindset. In fact, one of my go-to quotes during my keynotes is by Viktor Frankl, Holocaust survivor:

The last of human freedoms is the ability to choose one's attitude in any given set of circumstances.

The issue at hand is that we get so caught up in positivity that we deny a sense of realism. Life is tough. It's tougher for some than others. The objective of promoting empathy is to elevate others and promote emotional wellness, rather than abandoning, shaming, guilting, and excluding the less positive from healthy social circles. We are all responsible, even when it's not our fault. What we do next or don't do next is a choice.

With great power comes great responsibility.

This quote has been attributed to many: Voltaire, Winston Churchill, and Franklin D. Roosevelt. It's even been attributed to Spiderman.

When you are in a positive state of mind, do you find yourself staying away from negative people?

1. It's important to set boundaries for your own wellbeing, however, do you take a moment to understand what that person might be going through before distancing yourself? There is no right or wrong answer other than you not being honest with yourself.
2. Are you sensitive and aware as what you expect from people when you are not feeling positive due to something challenging that's happened, or is happening in your life?
3. Compare your answers from questions 1 and 2. Adjust your behavior and mindset accordingly if you feel a need for change.

Chapter 28

Hope and Optimism

The good news is that empathy can be developed. We can learn to be happy and positive, yet emotionally aware of the emotional needs of others. As a bonus, empathy can be implemented on the self. In fact, I encourage you to gift yourself with it. Some will call that self-love. I prefer the term self-care.

Self-Love???

Self-love focuses on the thoughts and feelings we have of ourselves. The very term, "self-love" defines the story of Narcissus. He's a Greek mythological character who looks into a river, sees his reflection and falls in love with his own beauty. The mental disorder of narcissism derives from Narcissus' legacy.

Self-care is about actions, such as nurturing the mind, body, and spirit.

Self-love promotes, "I, I, I, me, me, me," which is what narcissists do. They indulge in self-love to negate their empty, self-loathing egos. They "cum" first. In fact, the narcissist will emotionally climax knowing they have successfully and repeatedly deprived you of yours. The intention is inward and selfish. We have become an iSociety: "Follow ME. LIKE MY posts. Subscribe to MY channel. Selfies galore. Self-love promotes a narcissist mindset. It's emotional masturbation that is trending IMO. Social media reinforces this sense of self-love as an accepted modern standard. Ironically, the self-love mantra often disguises how much many dislike themselves.

Love is about giving and sharing something of such beauty with another. It is the universal frequency that was not designed to be about the self.

Self-care has a different intention. Action.

- ❖ *I will set boundaries because I respect and honor myself.*
- ❖ *I will get enough rest so I can be my best self.*
- ❖ *I will take me time to do what my soul needs.*

The difference between the two may appear to be a mere nuance based on semantics. It's a philosophical issue that I invite you to at least think about... even if only in the name of self-care.

Chapter 29

Because I'm Happy

Some people are genuinely happy, happy, happy. Some are somewhat happy and have learned that positive affirmations, law of attraction, and the power of manifestation will deliver the dream: money, love, success... "happiness".

The sad reality is, there are simply too many unhappy people in the world. You may find the following stats shocking.

Happiness in the workplace:
Gallup did a survey to measure employee engagement and happiness. They polled twenty-five million employees (part-time and full-time) in 189 different countries and concluded that one in two employees are not happy at work. That's a very sad statistic. People quit their bosses more than the job itself because their boss makes them unhappy. I think we can all relate to a bad boss who's made our lives miserable.

General happiness:
Source: TIME

- In a survey of 2,345 U.S. adults conducted online between April 10 and 15, 2013, only a third of Americans (33 percent) reported being very happy.

- People whose annual income is between $50,000 and $74,999 are happier than people who earn between $75,000 and $99,999.

- People with a college degree are happier than those without.
- The South is the happiest region.

- 65+ is the happiest age group.

- Married people are happier than unmarried.

- Having a child under the age of 18 in one's household makes no difference at all.

- People who are registered to vote are happier than average.

- People who live in the suburbs are generally happier than inner city dwellers.

Happiness by gender:
According to TIME magazine, women are happier than men.

Source: Wikigender

"Women report greater levels of unhappiness later in life compared to men, according to a new study conducted at the University of Cambridge and University of Southern California. (Published in the Journal of Happiness Studies 2008)."

Happiness by age:
Source: Wikigender

The same study showed that, "Men were the most melancholic at the age of 20, a period when they are most likely to be single. In contrast, greater life satisfaction for men is obtained through increasing purchasing power and the ability to acquire long-desired and coveted items, such as a car. These items might not be within their financial reach until later in life, explaining the increase in happiness."

"It was discovered that women are, on average, happier than men in early adulthood. The age of 48 seems to be an important turning point in women's sense of happiness, this is when there is a reversal in the fortunes and life satisfaction of the genders."

At the age of:

- ❖ **34:** Men's general satisfaction exceeds women's general satisfaction with life
- ❖ **41:** Men's financial satisfaction exceeds women's financial satisfaction
- ❖ **48:** Men's overall happiness exceeds women's overall happiness

- ❖ **64:** Men's satisfaction with family life exceeds women's satisfaction

Happiness by race:
Source: Huffington Post

- ❖ 28% of Hispanic Americans say they are happy.

- ❖ 36% of African Americans qualify as very happy.

- ❖ 34% of White Americans claim to be happy.

Empathy invites vulnerability.
Vulnerability inspires deep connection.
We are living in a highly disconnected world.
A world that craves empathy.

Chapter 30

Reaching Higher

Shared empathy is the emotional fuel that inspires people to take off and fly. It is the shield that protects you from dissociation and a sense of loneliness. Even the toughest among us, the stoics, the heartless, the numb, and the indifferent need empathy from somebody.

Imagine a world where more people were encouraged and inspired to fly or reach higher? Imagine a world where you were seen, heard, and understood by those you love, respect, work for, or look up to. In other words, we desire to be acknowledged by those we value. Imagine a world where we all experience deep connections, trust, and the high-frequency vibration of love. Imagine a world with the mindset of the Babembe Tribe in South Africa.

The pain of rejection from not being seen, respected, or understood by somebody you love manifests as physical pain. Your heart literally aches. Your nervous system goes into fight, flight, freeze, or fawn mode. Stress levels can go up, turning into anxiety and depression. Common consensus is we should not be impacted by how others view or treat us and that happiness comes from within. Well...

- Humans are social beings.
- Humans are emotional beings.

These two factors preordain the need for acceptance and belonging. Life is not designed for emotional masturbation. And when we do emotionally masturbate for too long, we experience an emotional deficit which quickly becomes a mental health issue.

For those who are happy, it's easy to say happiness comes from within. Their happiness means they have their needed elements to feel fulfilled, safe, and loved. It's kind of like being poor and hearing a rich person say that money isn't everything. It may not be everything, but it sure does play a massive role in our wellbeing.

"Happiness is not something you postpone for the future; it is something you design for the present."

Jim Rohn

That's the negative impact of being undermined, invisible, or disenfranchised on a collective scale. It hurts and breaks souls over time. If you deny that hurt, it will slowly creep up on you and turn into a serious mental health problem.

One of the saddest things I've witnessed over my fifty-seven years of life experience is witnessing human potential go to waste simply because a certain person neither had the tools, nor was supported. We should all be encouraged to reach higher. We can all reach higher. Maybe more importantly we have the power to help others reach higher, if not fly without a net.

I spoke earlier of the bad boss... that equates to a bad friend, a bad lover, a bad parent or sibling etc. We are all leaders in some capacity. Don't be the bad leader who dulls the light. A light that the world needs more than ever. Empowering and understanding others makes you a high-value person. It makes you a leader who makes a significant and positive difference.

Empathy is a superpower that elevates others. It connects us on a deep level. There is nothing more valuable to a human than to feel connected--the deeper the level, the more powerful and beautiful it is. Sadly, our current world is so disconnected. We are emotionally deprived and crave belonging. We have never been so lonely. Suicide is on the up. Depression is on the rise. General mental wellness is at an all-time high. We are in crisis... because the world lacks empathy. We have become an "I" generation rather than a "we" society.

———

Pink is more than a color. It's a mindset.

Chapter 31
Conflict Resolution

Almost every single relationship will eventually experience disagreement. Unresolved disagreements can fester over time, inspiring resentment. If this is left unaddressed, it usually means the demise of that relationship, sometimes getting ugly. Resentment can invite the ugly in the most beautiful, caring, patient and understanding humans. We all have a hint of Dr. Jekyll and Mr. Hyde in us.

Most conflicts occur due to four main reasons.

13. **Poor communication**: issues aren't clearly stated or aren't stated upfront, leaving a door to confusion and misinterpretation. It can be a question of pertinent information was emitted or vaguely stated. Good communication tends to be succinct and concise. Too much, or irrelevant information can distract from the point at hand diluting the message.

14. **Misunderstanding**: this doesn't necessarily mean poor communication. The challenge is the gap between what was said, even if appeared to be clear from the sender, and what was received. George Bernard Shaw, once said, "The greatest problem with communication is the illusion it has been accomplished."
15. **Unmet expectations**: this can be a question of a person not establishing expectations. This can invite disappointment, which can quickly become frustration.
16. **Boundaries that are violated**: this is potentially the easiest conflict agent to avoid. If a boundary was clearly expressed, but the other person fails to acknowledge or honor it, then the seeds of resentment will have been planted. Each time the boundary is not honored, due to misunderstanding or blatant disregard, the other person will feel violated.

The best way to avoid conflict is to avoid it. It sounds redundant, yet we tend to rarely focus on the elements that lead up to it. We are then left with conflict resolution to save the day.

Let's begin with how to avoid conflict.

There's a great customer service story about an angry airplane customer. It involves a woman on a JetBlue flight. I wish I knew who to give credit to for this powerful anecdote.

The entertainment screen of said woman isn't working... already frustrating. Adding fuel to her situation, she notices that the screen of the person seated next to her is working. She tells the flight attendant. He dismisses her by saying, "Ma'am there's nothing I can do about it." His reasoning in his head is that the flight is hectic. He's trying to get the flight off the ground on time. The lady got even more angry.

"This is not acceptable! How can I be on a four-hour flight without an entertainment system.?"

And that's when the "fight" started.

Why did she get angrier?

She got angrier because the flight attendant chose the wrong token. During all and any customer conflict (or personal conflict) situations, we each have the choice between two tokens.

Jean-Louis Gassier, who used to run Apple, France, says, "When customers are upset you have a choice between two tokens:

1. The first is: "It's not a big deal token."

2. The second is: "It's the end of the world token."

Because the flight attendant chose the first: "It's the not a big deal," token," the customer chose the second, "It's the end of the world," token and she got angrier.

If the flight attendant had chosen the "It's the end of the world token" because it was to the lady, it would've sounded like this… "I'm so sorry, I get frustrated too when entertainment screens don't work, especially on long flights. If you'd like, I can see if there are any available seats, I can move you to. In the interim, I can bring you some snacks that we reserve for a first-class customer.

If the flight attendant had chosen the second token, "It's the end of the world token," the customer would've chosen the, it's not a big deal token. If the first token is offered, but the customer still makes a scene, chances are that customer is an asshole.

Whenever anybody gets angry or frustrated with you, you have those same two choices.

1. It's the end of the world token. OR

2.   It's no big deal token.

Choose wisely and you will avoid conflicts.

So, what happens when it's too late and the conflict has erupted.

Here is a fantastic strategy to remember and use to resolve all and any conflicts. Btw, this an easy to remember and implement strategy. It works incredibly well at home and works wonders in the workplace with unhappy customers.

To be successful, the order of delivery must be in the order of the acronym, H.E.A.R.T

> **Hear**
> **Empathize**
> **Apologize**
> **Respond**
> **Thank**

HEAR: Take the time to hear what they have to say. Do nothing more than to simply listen. Instinctually, we tend to apologize immediately. Apologizing first is highly ineffective. Hold that thought.

EMPATHIZE: Because you have allowed them to get the frustration off their chest, there is emotional and mental relief. It is at this moment that we must express empathy. Do not apologize yet! Revert to chapter 27 (Empathy Sounds Like).

APOLOGIZE: It's possible that in their frustration while sharing the situation (venting/dumping), they won't hear your apology. They will later claim, "And can you believe it, they never even apologized." It's possible you apologized multiple times. While angry, we rarely acknowledge what people say, let alone hear an apology.

Secondly, how you can you be sorry if you don't understand my discomfort or inconvenience. They need to know you get it.

The apology can be tough to do well. It must be sincere. Saying, "I'm sorry you feel that way," is not an apology. A true and effective apology takes ownership of the situation. This means accountability and responsibility. Do not divert or deflect. Leave that to the narcissists. A good apology sounds something like this: "I apologize for…" Be very specific as to what you are sorry about. The ultimate apology is changed behavior.

RESPOND: As a result of your empathy and sincere apology, the odds are high that their frustration has been minimized. You are now in a great position to resolve the conflict. There are two options here.

The first is to let them know what you can do with the sole purpose to make it up to them. For example, I can put your steak order in again and for the inconvenience of waiting, can I offer you an additional glass of wine on the house? Get creative and work within the guidelines of you company. Hopefully they empower you to do what's best for the situation in the moment.
The second is to ask them what would make this situation better. You'll be surprised as to how fair and reasonable most people are, if you've heard, empathized and apologized.

THANK: You may wonder why we thank them. We thank them because they brought it to our attention, giving us an opportunity to fix it, learn and grow, rather than slander our brand reputation on social media and review platforms.

Again, the H.E.A.R.T acronym works wonders at home next time you leave the toilet seat up, (or down).

Chapter 32

Connection and Higher Consciousness

Did I mention that empathy not only changes lives, it saves lives? How do I know? Because it saved mine. It's what enabled me to dig my way out of the lowest of lows, the darkest of darks. And I know that I am not alone to have navigated this drab gauntlet.

Receiving empathy from only one person is potentially not enough. The average human needs to be seen and understood by more than one person. They say it takes a village, well, it really does.

Even the introverts and loners who love their solitude, need some sense of connection. For some, a dog/cat is enough to survive, but perhaps not enough to thrive. We aren't here on planet Earth to survive. I firmly believe that life is not that basic. On a higher consciousness level, we are all connected--with love being the vibration that gives us wings.

Unfortunately, love is not the only vibration we experience. To fully appreciate love and all that it encompasses, we must experience its antithesis: Yin Yang.

Harmony is not the absence of dark or evil. Sir Isaac Newton's third law says, "For every action, there is an equal and opposite reaction." So, there must be dark for the light to exist. There must be hate for love to exist. That is harmony. Harmony ceases to be when one element overwhelms the other. Empathy keeps human life in harmony, minimizing the selfishness, greed, and abusive nature of many human beings. It is the ultimate equalizer. It eradicates hate: homophobia, racism, sexism, anti-Semitism, and all the other forms of oppression, bigotry, conscious/unconscious bias and their evil step-twin, confirmation bias, where we twist reality to fit our beliefs.

Empathy brings us together. Empathy helps us connect, and we are so disconnected as a species.

Chapter 18
Love Language

Feeling, or having empathy, is one thing; communicating it is another. It is highly likely that the root cause of all failed relationships is poor communication. Many are insensitive in their communication skills, unable to meet the needs and expectations of their loved ones, romantic partners, friends, family, and colleagues.

Misunderstandings trigger resentment. Resentment builds up over time at each failed interaction or exchange of words and energy.

Barriers go up, distances increase. And then one day, we wake up wondering what happened.

As a keynote speaker, life coach, and leadership facilitator, I've created and delivered communication trainings for Fortune 100 and Fortune 500 companies. The same challenges repeat in all aspects of relationships both at home and at work. The fix is simple though not easy.

Here are a few basic insights and action steps that will help you improve your communication skills and invite healthy relationships that have a deeper connection--rapport.

It's possible you are familiar with Albert Merhabian. He's best known for his psychological analysis of communication. He breaks it down into two basic categories: Verbal and Non-verbal. Here are the percentages of our communication.

WORDS – 7%
BODY LANGUAGE – 55%
NON-VERBAL (facial expressions/tone of voice) – 38%

I borrow from his extensive research and wisdom, adding a few components my exploration has led me to conclude.

There are six basic communication pillars that I address. I borrow them from my online communication course titled "Reaching Higher Through Communication."

1. LISTENING
2. BODY LANGUAGE
3. TONE OF VOICE /FACIAL EXPRESSIONS
4. WORDS
5. ENERGY
6. INTENTION

Empathy is a love language.

Each one of these six pillars can be fueled by empathy or not. When they are, communication becomes much more effective, inspiring deeper understanding and connection.

Here is a beautiful and healthy communication platform I learned from a TED Talk by Julien Treasure. I share this at my keynotes and trainings with great impact. It's based on an easy to remember acronym.

HAIL

H is for **honesty**... be clear and straight.
A is for **authenticity**... be yourself
I is for **integrity**... be your word.
L is for **love**... not romantic love, love in the sense of wishing them well, void of judgment.

If you are able to implement the HAIL concept into your communication, so much will change. You will be communicating with empathy.

The one element I'm going to add to the HAIL acronym is V for vulnerability.

Vulnerability is a very powerful way of inviting deep connection. It means you're putting down your walls and truly allowing somebody in. Share your story. It will open a door for them to do the same. Then listen with empathy. When I talk about vulnerability, I don't mean sharing sob stories or complaining. It's more about sharing a challenge you face or have overcome; it's about sharing something personal. It takes courage to be vulnerable. It's definitely not a weakness. Leverage Emotional Intelligence to gauge what to share, how much to share and when to share it.

PINK IS THE COLOR OF EMPATHY

Becoming a high-value person in a disconnected world

I believe empathy is the most essential quality of civilization.

Roger Ebert

As a society, we must dig much deeper into the meaning and objective of true empathy.

Chapter 34
Types of Empathy

We must be more aware and analytical of our behaviors and levels of listening and understanding to pains and burdens which are not ours. Because, once it becomes about us in the slightest, it is no longer empathy, but rather a comparison disguised with the mask of sympathy. That is not empathy.

As a society, we must dig much deeper into the meaning and objective of true empathy. There are in fact four types of empathy:

1. **Cognitive empathy:** The ability to understand how a person feels and what they might be thinking. Cognitive empathy improves our communication skills, because we

become sensitive and aware of how we can best reach and connect to another person. The narcissist can have this empathic ability which they leverage for harm.

2. **Emotional empathy** (affective empathy): The ability to share the feelings of another person. Think of it as "your pain in my heart." If their pain is in your heart, you have probably built a very strong, secure and deep connection with that person. Well played.

3. **Compassionate empathy** (empathic concern): This is more about taking action than just feeling.

4. **Directional empathy**: This is the highest level of empathy. It allows you to move through the world and know what's coming toward you energetically and emotionally.

Chapter 35
Getting Really Deep

During the filming of "Old," director M. Night Shyamalan honored ancient wisdom and demonstrated empathy at such a deep and universal level.

Going back to the word "respect," in an earlier chapter, as the consummate form of empathy because it means "seeing the person," which can also come in the form of acknowledgement or gratitude. But wait, there's more.

The ancients often demonstrated empathy through rituals that honored the circle of life and nature in general. When they hunt, they kill a beast and offer thanks for what that animal will provide them and for the loss of that animal. They understand the suffering of that animal, while honoring nature--life and death for the purpose of survival. The most "primitive" tribes did not kill for pleasure or sport. That involves a total lack of empathy for the animal, and empathy is not limited to one's own kind but to every living creature on planet earth.

Don't worry, I am not promoting veganism or imposing any judgment on you for eating or not eating meat. In fact, I love meat, despite becoming more conscious recently and cutting back. However, I won't eat lobster. The thought of boiling a creature while it's alive is too much for me. We all draw the line in the sand at a different place. I honor my line and respect where yours is. It's simply about being mindful for what was lost and honoring the suffering for our own gain.

M. Night Shyamalan was faced with natures challenge during "Old." The shoot schedule fell smack during hurricane season. It meant heavy rains and wind that would impact the visual of their semi-designed isolated beach. The crew had to learn to understand and honor nature's behavior. The elements would wash away the beach, setting filming challenges. They smartly adapted and worked with nature rather than against it.

The Ottomans build bird watering holes on the wall of their buildings and other elements to maintain as much harmony with nature as possible. We have so much to learn.

Respect is shared in a multitude of ways, as is empathy, and they are not limited to humans, rather with all of nature. Nature as a collective is a living entity that warrants the same type of empathy and respect. Is global warming a consequence of humankind's lack of empathy toward the planet that is our home? I leave that up to you.

We must "see" and acknowledge the universe and nature rather than control, defy or rape it. *Sawubona* Mother Nature ((Zulu for "I see you").

Respect (honor acknowledgment) is the ultimate human/life flex.

Empathy does not equate to agreement. It also doesn't mean that you condone another's behaviors, core values or beliefs.

Chapter 34

What Really Matters In The End

The last words of Steve Jobs, billionaire, dead at 56:

"I have reached the summit of success in the world of business." In the eyes of others, my life is a success. However, aside from work, I had little joy. In the end, wealth is just a fact I am used to. At this moment, laying on my hospital bed, remembering my whole life, I realize that all the gratitude and wealth in which I took so much pride, has vanished and became meaningless in the face of imminent death.

You can hire someone to drive your car or make money for you but it's impossible to hire someone to deal with sickness and die for you. Material things lost can be found. But there is one thing that can never be found when it is lost - "Life". Whatever stage of life we are currently in, with time, we will face it the day the curtain closes. Love your family, spouse, and friends... Treat them right. Cherish them.

As we get older, and wiser, we slowly realize that wearing a $300 or $30 watch - both give the same hour...

Whether we have a $300 or $30 wallet or purse - the amount inside is the same; Whether we drive a $150,000 car or $30,000 car, the road and distance are the same, and we arrive at the same destination. That we drink a bottle of wine at $1000 or $10 hangover is the same; That the house we live in is 300 or 3000 square feet - the loneliness is the same. You will realize that your true inner happiness does not come from material things of this world.

Whether you travel first class or economic class, if the plane crashes, you crash with it... Therefore... I hope you realize, when you have friends, boyfriends and old friends, brothers and sisters, with whom you argue, laugh, talk, sing, talk about north-south-east or heaven and earth,.... This is the real happiness!!

An indisputable fact of life:

Don't educate your kids to be rich. Educate them to be happy. So when they grow up they will know the value of things and not the price."

Here are nine ways to gauge your social worth.

1. Be authentic, respectful, and kind in the way you show up.
2. Communicate with love and sincerity.
3. Determine and live by your core values.
4. Be impeccable with your word.
5. Be clear and honorable with your intentions and purpose.
6. Have more empathy, with healthy boundaries.
7. Show people you care.
8. Giving back or paying it forward.
9. Be a safe person (trustworthy / non-judgmental).

Society is emotionally struggling, in particular, the younger generations who need more emotional support than actual financial resources or celebrity.

As a parent, as a friend, lover, or partner, be the best version of you for that person and you instantly become a high-value person. The best example I can think of, is a teacher. They rarely become financially wealthy; they are underpaid heroes! Yet, a good teacher brings infinite value to the next generation. I can think of one or two of my teachers who heavily influenced the course of my life, if not saved my life growing up as a kid lost in the British Child Care System. Their value was and is priceless.

Take a moment to self-evaluate.

As a person, are you doing that little extra and being the best version of yourself with the wellbeing of others at heart? If yes, you are a high-value person. Congrats.

As a leader, are you inspiring and empowering your team? If you are, then you instantly become a high-value leader. If you work at the register at Walmart, are you committed to providing great customer service to each and every person you ring up? If you are, then you are a high-value person.

Have the mindset to want to reach higher every day, the mindset to do more for your village or community, the mindset to be more empathetic, to be more giving and caring etc. That is wealth right there.

If you are an influencer to the masses but provide little value to those who really need you--your kids, your significant other, etc.-- then consider shifting the focus to those who really love you, not only those who admire you without knowing you. Ultimately, do that little extra and optimize who you are and become not only a high-value person, but an extraordinary person. How to become your best self? Discover your **IKIGAI**.

Former Miami Dolphins head coach, Jimmy Johnson, once said, "The difference between ordinary and extraordinary, is that little extra."

The choice is yours.

———

What really matters most to you at this time in your life?

1. Are you investing in, and nurturing what matters most to you?
2. Could you do, and give more?
3. What needs to change if anything?
4. How will you implement this mindset change?
5. What is the expected or desired outcome?

Pink is also the color of
Emotional Intelligence--
the sophisticated word
for empathy. Pink is also the color
of being woke, the urban term for
Emotional Intelligence
(being considerate, understanding
and caring).

Chapter 35
Deserving

Giving empathy or being empathetic can be emotionally draining. You may have heard about the social struggles of empaths who easily get depleted in social settings because they feel too much and absorb external energy.

When extending empathy, protect your energy and emotional wellness by setting boundaries with the person in search of understanding. Set boundaries for yourself, too... how much can you give, how long can you listen before it becomes detrimental to you.

Prolonged empathy can become toxic; you become a potential enabler, or you inspire trauma bonding, which isn't really a win-win scenario. Know your limits. Everything in moderation.

I don't know if there is a scientific equation to determine who is the giver or the receiver. My recommendation is to offer empathy to anybody you feel needs it, or anybody who is asking for it, provided you are in a strong enough emotional state to give a part of your heart and mind to that person. Empathy is giving which can drain. It's usually the person in a position of confidence, emotional and mental fortitude, who cares, who can, should, and will extend empathy. In healthy relationships, the role will often change. Give and take as needed.

DAILY CHALLENGES OF BEING EMPATHETIC

We may think we are being empathetic with pure intentions, but we could be fooling ourselves. We may still be making it about us, sharing a related incident we experienced. This communicates relatability, but we must quickly shift the focus back to them and not divert the attention to us by hogging the conversation, which is easily, and all too often done.

We must fully commit to making it entirely about that other person's experience, perspective, and any additional circumstances they have endured for it to be true empathy. The trap is we are influenced by our own personal agenda, needs, and expectations. So, we listen with every intent to understand, but we still view if from our personal perspective and may offer advice (coaching), a pep talk, (cheerleading), and condemn them (negative judgment). All of which bring little value to the person in need of empathy. Instead, it makes us feel good about our positive mindset, our needs and expectations, or flexing the wisdom we have to resolve their problem.

Empathy is not necessarily about resolving. It's about feeling and being there in the way that that person needs you--which might be coaching or motivation, or simply listening and being present for them void of action. A good suggestion to truly help is to ask the person, "How can I be of value?"

I believe that if we took the time and committed to truly being empathetic, we could and would eradicate, hate, racism, sexism, phobias, social disconnect, depression, violence, crime, and judgment in general.

Unfortunately, constant empathy is not possible. I recommend strategic doses as we progressively expand our minds and open our hearts to that which we don't fully grasp. We must trust in the other person's perspective and experience as truth, void of imposing anything about us into that conversation or experience. If we can't commit to making it ALL ABOUT THEM, we will continue to invite conflict, alienation and isolation. Comparison with a sprinkle of sympathy thrown into the mix is not empathy. It's simply comparison with a sprinkle of sympathy.

All we can do is strive to become more effective with our empathy through awareness of the self, others and our environment (Emotional Intelligence).

Empathy is the highest form of intelligence. - Anthony Gucciardi

<u>Bill Bullard</u> went one step further than Gucciardi when he said, "Opinion is really the lowest form of human knowledge. It requires no accountability, no understanding. The highest form of knowledge… is empathy, for it requires us to suspend our egos and live in another's world. It requires profound purpose larger than the self-kind of understanding."

———

When you show deep empathy toward others, their defensive energy goes down, and positive energy replaces it. That's when you can get more creative in solving problems.

Stephen Covey

Chapter 35
The Garden Of Good And Evil

Like all human traits and abilities, they can be used for good or for evil.

The gift of empathy can in fact be a highly dangerous and powerful skill when it comes to the dark arts of manipulation. Part of the reason for its stealthy and sorrowful seductiveness is that people simply don't see it coming. They don't see it coming because it's so well cloaked in goodness. We assume that somebody who is empathetic understands us, so they are a friend. FALSE. Not always.

A cunning empath can be as harmful as a narcissist who allegedly lacks empathy. The only difference between the two is that the narcissist doesn't know, feel, or understand guilt, shame, remorse, or regret. The sneaky and slimy empath, knows all too well, and simply continues, anyway.

Remember, empathy is the highest form of intelligence. And that, is power, good and/or bad.

The choice reminds me of the story of the 2 wolves:

One evening an old Cherokee told his grandson about a battle that goes on inside people.

He said, "My son, the battle is between two wolves inside us all.

One is evil: it is anger, envy, jealousy, sorrow, regret, greed, arrogance, self-pity, guilt, resentment, inferiority, lies and ego.

The other is good: It is joy, peace, love, hope, humility, benevolence, empathy, generosity, truth, compassion, kindness and faith."

The grandson thought about it for a moment and then asked, "Grandfather, which wolf wins?"

The old Cherokee smiled and simply said,

PINK IS THE COLOR OF EMPATHY

Becoming a high-value person in a disconnected world

"The one you feed."

Chapter 36

Sawubona

I hope you choose the superpower of empathy for good. Empathy not only changes lives, it saves lives.

The beauty and power of empathy come through the giving and communicating of empathy. Make sure that your empathetic generosity establishes healthy boundaries to honor YOU, too.

Know thyself. Know others by seeing them. Become a high-value person in a world that is often too cold, indifferent and disconnected. Let's connect by seeing each other, even when our thinking and beliefs are different.

Sawubona (I see you).

Take a moment to evaluate the mindset and
emotional state of those people in your close circle.

When was the last time you genuinely took the time to see
somebody and maybe ask
how they were doing? And I don't mean
on a casual level. I mean, having an intimate
moment with them fueled by caring, vulnerability, and an
overload of empathy.

I challenge you to choose
one or two people this week and
share more empathy.

Be more curious as to who
they are and how they are doing deep down. The key to
succeeding in this endeavor is to establish a safe and trusting
connection. This may take time to build.
Copy, paste, repeat... and repeat, and repeat.

Chapter 37

Why Pink?

The story behind pink is quite interesting, if not surprising. Like all colors, there are emotional, vibrational, and spiritual qualities attached or associated to them.

As a consensus, pink is the sweet side of red. It has been considered to represent the following:

> **Friendship**
> **Affection**
> **Harmony**
> **Inner Peace**
> **Approachability**

On a religious level (according to the meaning of colors in the Bible--not that I subscribe to the Bible), pink is associated with:

> **New Life**
> **Healthy flesh** (oh, oh... racially controversial and potentially bias perspective of skin tones and wellness)
> **Heavenly care**
> **The feminine**
> **The Rose of Sharon** (Hibiscus Syriacus) is a pink flower with a red center. It means love, healing, and beauty.

Regarding color psychology it is a color of hope. It also calms and sooths our emotions, minimizing aggression, resentment, and anger.

Pink has even been leveraged in prisons. A series of studies led by research scientist Alexander Schauss showed that pink pacified people. This inspired prison wardens to test the theory in the 1980s. Holding cells were painted pink. It had to be a specific shade and intensity of pink. Schauss named the perfect pink after Naval correctional institute directors Baker and Miller. It's called Baker-Miller Pink. This color lowered the number of assaults between inmates. Some sports coaches have even been known to paint the lockers of the visiting team pink to pacify their opponents. I'm calling foul play on that one.

The wrong pink would have the opposite effect. It would inspire aggression.

When and why did pink become associated with girls?

The 19th Century is when the genders became color coded. Prior to that, all babies were dressed in white dresses. Historian, Jo B. Paoletti, says the that the reason for white was purely practical. White cotton was easily bleached. Dresses (worn until the age of six) allowed for quick and easy diaper change.

The onset of the 20th Century introduced the use of pastel colors, in particular, blue and pink. Gender roles had not yet been assigned to each color. The trade publication *Earnshaw's Infants' Department* declared in 1918 that the "generally accepted rule is pink for the boys, and blue for the girls. The reason is that pink, being a more decided and stronger color (close to red), is more suitable for the boy, while blue, which is more delicate and daintier, is prettier for the girl."

That didn't stick and sales of children's clothing suffered. An intentional rebrand saved the day. So, today's use of pink for girls and blue for boys is by marketing design. In 1946 Baby Boomers fully adopted this notion. It stuck.

Due to the many connotations of what pink has meant historically, it makes great sense for modern branding colors by gender to be determined by the feminine qualities of pink. It is for these nurturing and gentle qualities that I chose pink as the color of empathy.

———

Chapter 38 (bonus)
Neurodivergence

I consider the empath to belong within the group labelled, neurodivergent. Empaths are not neurotypical.

The general understanding of neurodivergent is predominantly associated with people who are on the autism spectrum. It also includes anybody whose brain functions differently.

This is what the Cleveland Clinic has to say about the neurodivergent.

*PART 1: The term "neurodivergent" describes people whose brain differences affect how their brain works. That means they have different strengths and **challenges** from people whose brains don't have those differences. The possible differences include medical **disorders**, learning **disabilities** and other **conditions**.*

It's a polite, politically correct term "they" give to those "they" view is mentally f%&*@d up.

PART 2: The possible strengths include better memory, being able to mentally picture three-dimensional (3D) objects easily, the ability to solve complex mathematical calculations in their head, and many more.

Society tends to only register Part 1... the disorders, challenges or "conditions".

If we focus on Part 2, we realize that neurodivergence is a gift, a superpower that is above the norm.

Society likes to keep people in alignment with the lowest common denominator for the sake of control and/or assimilation into the set standards of an outdated education system designed to create conforming worker-bees. And btw, the Empath and HSP are forms of neurodivergence.

Let's take Part 2 to a different level, starting with so-called ailments and disorders such as **ADD** (Attention Deficit Disorder). Just because the average person lacks curiosity and intrigue and is almost numbed by mass hypnosis and made placid in thought, doesn't mean that the highly **curious** have a disorder. Rather than medicate and numb brain, put them more challenging and creative environments, or teach them mediation. As far as I am concerned, lacking curiosity is a disorder. Ask Albert Einstein, who once said, "I have no special talents, I am only passionately curious". Passionately curious!

Let's take ADHD (Attention Deficit Hyperactivity Disorder), in short, overly active with heightened spontaneity. Is that really a disorder, compared to being an emotionally numb drone of middle society? Encourage and inspire them to choose careers that require more energy and quick decision-making. This is a rudimentary suggestion that requires deeper thinking and exploration, but without that deeper exploration, prescriptions and shaming aren't really solving the "problem".

The list of diagnosed disorders as acronyms is endless. And btw, almost all of them are recent phenomenon or labels with a negative connotation. How are they treated? With pharmaceuticals that make them act like everybody else. Hmmm. How are they created? Arguably pharmaceuticals for financial gain by obligating people to be on life-time medication. Genius.

Perhaps we should embrace and elevate this exceptional people rather than condemn and banish them to an inferior status guilted into shame as if they have cerebral cooties.

So, let's talk about the disorder of being highly sensitive (HSP). Again, this is not a disorder. It's a gift, as superpower, as is autism and ADD etc. Think Rain Man (movie with Dustin Hoffman and Tom Cruise. Dustin Hoffman's character has extraordinary mathematical abilities... "they" consider that a disorder... LMAO.

If you fall into the category of a neurodivergent, in any, and all of its numerous variations: Depersonalization/Derealization Disorder (DPDRD); Other Specified Dissociative Disorders (OSDD); Unspecified Dissociative Disorder (UDD) etc, etc... including the empath, the psychic, or Rain man/women), begin celebrating your unique gifts and end the shame. You are special. You are magical. You have a superpower. I honor you!

Sawubona.

THE END

PINK IS THE COLOR OF EMPATHY

Becoming a high-value person in a disconnected world

Remember to have empathy for YOU.

About the Author

Since leaving Cirque du Soleil, Vital Germaine started an entertainment production company that produced live events around the world. Many years later, following a newfound sense of purpose and passion, he started a consulting company called ENGAGEteams360.

Vital has become a reputable, dynamic, and engaging public speaker, corporate trainer, and transformation leader.

Vital delivers relevant, impactful, and transformational workshops, keynotes and trainings that inspire meaningful transformation.

For more information on Vital's books, products, and services log on to: VitalGermaine.com.

If you enjoyed the read, please leave a review on Amazon and share the book with a friend, colleague. If you didn't enjoy the read, recommend the book to an enemy.

Thank you.

Other books by Vital

FLYING WITHOUT A NET is partially about life in the amazing Cirque du Soleil. It is more a touching story filled with hope and belief. An inspirational story that defines the power of the human spirit. A spirit we all have.

The top-selling book has been called:

- o INSPIRATIONAL
- o A MUST READ.
- o STUNNING MEMOIR
- o COULDN'T PUT IT DOWN
- o BEST READ OF THE YEAR
- o READ COVER TO COVER IN ONE SITTING

Other books by Vital

FLYING WITHOUT A NET 2.0 is the sequel to FLYING WITHOUT A NET. If you are looking to overcome professional and personal challenges, soar and achieve more in life, then this book is for you. I

It's been called:

- A 10!
- CAPTIVATING. COMPELLING!
- EXTRAORDINARY!
- TRIUMPHANT. FIVE STARS!
- DIDN'T WANT IT TO END!
- WONDERFUL MUST READ
- POWERFUL, INSPIRATIONAL
- MUST READ. VERY INSPIRING.
- VITAL DID IT AGAIN!

Other books by Vital

INNOVATION MINDSET is designed for entrepreneurs, business owners, executives, leaders and cultures to be inspired and enabled to navigate change. It includes a series of action steps to simplify transformation. It will also have a positive impact on your personal life as you improve your problem-solving skills and confidence.

The book includes interviews with thought leaders from different industries: Tim Sanders, New York Times Best-selling author and former Yahoo executive.
Jordan Adler, Best-selling author and MLM Millionaire.
Randy Sutton, former police detective and TV News contributor.
Dennis Bonilla, former U.S. Navy Nuke!

It's been called:

- o Brilliant!
- o A must-have for your leadership library!
- o Calling all leaders. I highly recommend this book.
- o Interesting and entertaining, genius and genuine.
- o Definitely the inspiration I needed to venture outside my comfort zone and CREATE!
- o Great stories and illustrations of relevant and timely principles any leader, in any organization can apply to take their life and career to new heights.

Other books by Vital

REACHING HIGHER, 21 Ways To Keep Life Positive, is a quick and easy read to help lift your spirits on those slower days when you need more than a strong coffee to get you going.

It's been called:

- o Highly beneficial for everyone.
- o A beautiful collection of mindset reminders.
- o Get this NOW!
- o Uplifted and encouraged
- o Inspiring

Other books by Vital

3 SIMPLE STEPS is a short - childlike story written for adults who are on a journey of growth and healing. Be inspired. Feel compelled to overcome and reach higher. Follow the journey of a young student whose future is forever changed when a teacher reveals the magic and wisdom of a journal an elder once shared.

A charming coffee table book for a rainy day when the desire to design a better life becomes apparent. It's been called:

- o   BRAVO
- o   ENJOY BEING INSPIRED
- o   IT REALLY GOT MY ATTENTION
- o   SUPER FUN LITTLE BOOK
- o   YOU'll READ IT OVER AND OVER AGAIN

Other books by Vital

#1 New Best Seller
THINK LIKE AN ARTIST is a simple, fun, yet profound look into creativity as a human superpower. In this short book, you'll discover how to leverage and optimize your life by shifting your mindset to one of growth and opportunity. Whilst along the journey, you'll be intrigued by the mystical, captivating, and powerful narrative of my 5 years in, Mesdames et Messieurs, Le Cirque du Soleil, as an acrobat and team captain. Learn about the process of turning good into great through the spirit of risk, adventure and achievement. You won't be the same person by the end.

Connect with me @TheSigmaEmpath
or VitalGermaine

Dear empath, kind-hearted soul, indigo baby, flower child, caring spirit, healer, light-worker, and nurturer, though it may sometimes feel like a burden, remember that your sensitivity, kindness, caring, awareness (emotional intelligence) and light, is a gift...
a superpower.

Thank you.

Printed in Great Britain
by Amazon